CUSTARD

THE LANGHAM

AFTERNOON TEA BOOK

WHITE LION
PUBLISHING

THE LANGHAM
LONDON

FOREWORD BY MICHEL ROUX JR

The moment I set foot inside The Langham, at its iconic original venue on Portland Place, I knew it was the only hotel in London I wanted to partner with. We share the same values and passion for creating lasting memories. That relationship is now more than fifteen years old, and over that time I have developed not only a deep appreciation for the hotel group's ethos – whether that's in London or elsewhere in the world – but also for its unparalleled, legendary afternoon tea!

I was only sixteen when I gained an apprenticeship in Paris under Master Pâtissier Henri Hellegouarch. My father and uncle had told me that if I wanted follow in their footsteps and become a chef, the creativity and science of pâtisserie was the perfect place to start. And, indeed, it was. The exquisite touches that you see in delicate cakes and pastries – from the flavour combinations to the decoration and presentation – are the epitome of all wonderful cooking: layering, precision, beauty and art. As a guest, the enjoyment comes not just from the food preparation (a feast for all the senses) but in the service, the experience, the sense of indulgence too.

This book makes my mouth water – among the recipes are some of my absolute favourites. A sandwich of Roast Cauliflower and Gentlemen's Relish is pure delight, combining sweet and savoury and wrapped in pillowy, light bread. I love the playful aspects of The Langham's afternoon tea: Custard Cream has all the hallmarks of the great, classic biscuit; it is delicious and nostalgic – but it is definitely not one for dunking. Among the sharing cakes, the Honey Cake is perhaps the most perfect afternoon-tea treat you could wish for... but I should confess that it is so irresistible I have also been known to have a slice for breakfast!

I hope these and others in the book reveal something of the genius it takes for our chefs to create Afternoon Tea at The Langham. Above all, though, whether you are here simply to remember and cherish your own experience with us, or to feel inspired to take out your scales and re-create some of these amazing recipes at home, I invite you to the table with the same sense of excitement and belonging that I felt when I arrived at The Langham all those years ago. Brew yourself a perfect cup, sit with us, and enjoy.

ABOVE
Brigade de Cuisine,
The Langham, London
c.1907

LEFT
The kitchens were state
of the art in the 1920s

OUR STORY

The origin of afternoon tea is unclear. Anna, the seventh Duchess of Bedford, is most often credited with the idea of having a tray of sandwiches, cakes and scones brought to her rooms to stave off a 'sinking feeling' that would come on in the hours between lunch and dinner. And why not? We all know the feeling of needing something to pep us up mid-afternoon and see us through until supper. For those with the means, the notion quickly caught on and a new afternoon ritual found its home in early Victorian society. The foundations were set: a social occasion as much as a meal; a chance to slow down, catch up and to see and be seen.

More than the sum of its parts, the afternoon tea is an occasion – it is a cherished British tradition, from the cucumber sandwiches to the scones and clotted scream, all steeped in elegance, artistry and timeless ritual. Where the Full English Breakfast and the Sunday Roast emerge as family traditions of hard-working British people, the afternoon tea is a cultural emblem of ceremony, grace and refinement.

If the origin of afternoon tea remains uncertain, what we do know is that when the then Prince of Wales opened The Langham, London, on 10th June 1865, he called this newest of Europe's Grand Hotels 'a fine hotel... everything a man, woman or child could desire, all under one roof'. Alongside Breakfast, Luncheon and Supper on the opening menu appears that most recent cultural addition: 'Teas: 1s 6d'.

The Langham's early adoption of the afternoon tea aligns with its other cutting-edge innovations. The Hotel offered its guests hydraulic elevators ('rising rooms'), hot and cold running water in en-suite bathrooms and, remarkable at the time, air-conditioning. Initially cooling only the Hotel's 30-metre by 12-metre restaurant, air-conditioning was, over time, installed throughout the Reading Rooms, Sitting Rooms and Drawing Rooms of the Ground Floor's public spaces and eventually into the (then) glass-ceilinged Palm Court. At the heart of the tea experience was this room, so named for the exotic palms and the light-filled space it housed. Its legacy as a social gathering place dates back to the hotel's opening when it welcomed the city's elite for conversation, gossip and – of course – tea. Today, it remains

THE LANGHAM HOTEL,

PORTLAND PLACE, W.

NOW OPEN

TARIFF.

Ground Floor.	s.	d.		s.	d.
Sitting-room and Bed-room …from	12	0	to	28	0
Bed-room … ,,	4	0	,,	8	0
First Floor					
Drawing-room, with Bed and Dressing-room, &c., *en suite* …	25	0	upwards.		
Drawing-room and Bed-room …	12	0	to	25	0
Sitting-rooms and Saloons…	8	0	,,	30	0
Bed-rooms …	3	6	,,	10	0
Second Floor.					
Drawing-room, with Bed and Dressing-room, &c., *en suite* …	20	0	,,	25	0
Drawing-room and Bed-room, *en suite* …				15	0
Sitting-rooms…				10	0
Bed-rooms and Dressing-room communicating	7	0	,,	15	0
Bed-rooms …	3	0	,,	10	6
Third Floor.					
Sitting-room, Bed, and Dressing-room, &c., *en suite* …	18	0	,,	21	0
Bed-room and Dressing-rooms, communicating	7	0	,,	12	0
Bed-rooms…	3	0	,,	8	0
Fourth Floor.					
Dressing-room and Bed-room, communicating..	5	6	,,	10	6
Bed-rooms…	2	6	,,	5	0

Upper Floor—BED-ROOMS, from 1*s.* 6*d.* to 2*s.* 6*d.*

Item	s.	d.
Extra Beds occupied on the First or Second Floors …	2	6
Ditto, on the Third or Fourth Floors…	2	0
Visitors' Servant's Bed, per night …	1	6
Ditto Board, per day (each) …	5	0
Children's Cots …	1	0
Baths.		
Hot Baths …	2	0
Cold…	1	0
Shower …	1	0
Hip or Sponge …		

Salle à Manger, or General Dining Room for Ladies and Gentlemen, 100 feet by 40 feet:—

Item	s.	d.
Breakfast, plain …	2	0
,, Cold Meat or Eggs…	2	6
,, Chops or Steaks, Broiled Ham and Eggs…	3	0
Teas, plain …	1	6
Dinner, off Joint…	2	6
,, à la Carte …		
Suppers and Luncheons…from	1	6
Cups of Tea or Coffee …	0	6

TABLE D'HOTE, 5*s.*

When Meals are supplied in Bed Rooms, 1*s.* per head extra will be charged.

The Hotel contains Ladies' elegant Sitting-room, Gentlemen's spacious Reading and Writing-room and well-ventilated Smoking-room.

Spacious suites of Apartments are especially reserved for Wedding Breakfasts, Dinner Parties, &c.

Service.—Visitors will be charged 1*s.* 6*d.* per day each. Casual Customers, 6*d.* each meal.

The Hotel Company will not be responsible for property lost in the Hotel; and, therefore, request Visitors to leave all valuables at the bar, accompanied with a written memorandum.

Visitors are requested not to pay any money without a bill.

Visitors giving up apartments are requested to give notice of their intention before noon.

The Manager will make special arrangements with Families engaging their apartments for a period.

Private Carriages of every description supplied, by the Day or Hour, at Fixed Charges.

COURIERS SUPPLIED IF REQUIRED.

*** Visitors are requested to communicate any cause of complaint to the Manager, that it may be immediately investigated and rectified.

C. SCHUMANN, Manager.

ABOVE
The Langham, London's opening menu from 10th June 1865

an essential part of London's cultural landscape, a place where locals will gather, as much as an historically significant meeting-place beloved of overseas visitors and other hotel guests.

From the very beginning Afternoon Tea at The Langham attracted the fashionable and the famous. In the early years, royalty mingled with literary greats; Mark Twain and Wilkie Collins were regulars. Over a meal in the drawing room, Sir Arthur Conan Doyle was commissioned to write the Sherlock Holmes novel *The Sign of Four* and Oscar Wilde *The Picture of Dorian Gray*. More than simply rooms or a place for events, Portland Place soon became a hub for inspiration, conversation and social display. Ladies in crinolines and gentlemen in top hats would gather to see and be seen – the hotel's hallways built especially wide to accommodate the wider dress style of the age.

As time passed, and the guest list moved from Emperor Napoleon III whiling away his time in exile to Noël Coward writing for inter-War theatre, so the menu and style for The Langham's Afternoon Tea evolved. By the turn of the last century, the hotel began to incorporate a more modish and refined French pâtisserie. When the lively and fashion-conscious post-War 1920s arrived, The Langham was enjoying a heyday – leading the hospitality world in the ways of luxury and opulence. By the 1930s, The Langham's ever-present Afternoon Tea service was accompanied by an ensemble of musicians who would go on to become the BBC's Palm Court Orchestra.

When the unthinkable happened and there was onset of a second World War, The Langham Hotel played its part. The hotel, through the BBC, hosted wartime broadcasts by British Prime Minister Winston Churchill and French General Charles de Gaulle. Once World War II was over, the hotel's role as a broadcasting house continued: it became an additional home for BBC studios, an extension of 1930s Broadcasting House on just the other side of the street. Then, eventually, in the late 1990s and early 2000s, the hotel was returned to its former splendour. Full-scale renovations, gloriously befitting of its historical significance, restored The Langham to the ranks of the top hotels in London.

'The Langham is still known as the spiritual home of Afternoon Tea – the first of the Grand Hotels to bring this tradition to life…'

The timeless elegance and enduring appeal of Afternoon Tea at The Langham means that, to this day, the experience remains a pillar of the hotel's identity. Afternoon Tea now is a celebration of heritage elevated with a modern sensibility.

With the group having expanded from the corner of Regent Street and Portland Place to Los Angeles and Chicago in the USA and Shanghai and Hong Kong in China, and as far as Sydney and Melbourne in Australia, you would be forgiven for thinking that the traditions of the Hotel's original London home might falter. However, while each season brings new ingredients and inventive interpretations, the essence of the experience – elegance, indulgence, and a time to pause and celebrate life's moments – remains intact wherever you are in the world. With more than 160 years of history poured into every cup, positioned on every cake stand and laid on to every plate, it is no surprise that The Langham is still known as the spiritual home of Afternoon Tea – the first of the Grand Hotels to bring this tradition to life beyond the walls of private houses.

The Langham, London

THE LANGHAM'S SIGNATURE STYLE

More than any other meal, an afternoon tea is an occasion. It is a dining experience elevated to an artform – a legacy of decades of ritual, classic elegance combined with contemporary flair. The magic ingredient comes somewhere intangibly among the food, the service and the ambience, which all play their part in creating a truly memorable event. No matter the pedigree and history of The Langham Afternoon Tea, nor how many pots of tea, or scones or sandwiches are served, each three-tiered stand is an opportunity to wow. When it arrives at the table, we know it is building lifelong memories for our guests.

While each of The Langham Hotels serves its own take on an Afternoon Tea, reflecting the local customs and traditions of its location, what truly defines The Langham experience is the artistry behind every plate and cup. That goes for the service, as well as the food. Overseen by our world-class chefs and service teams, the menus are precisely designed to indulge and captivate, from the finesse of the cakes and savouries to the serving of the cups of tea themselves.

Creating ambience

A blend of location, architecture and design, every Langham Hotel is unique in its character. Nonetheless, each location shares the common ambition to curate exceptional, memorable experiences for its guests. The lounge is always a rich, layered environment where textures, patterns and soft hues unfold in delicate harmony. Live music is a must, the soft tones enhancing the sense of occasion: wherever you are, there will always be a space reserved for a grand piano or a harp.

At the table, the mood and style of our Afternoon Tea is evoked through carefully curated table settings. Each hotel has a whole range of specific equipment, containers, vessels, plates and cutlery reserved exclusively for serving tea. Sterling silver cake forks, delicate jam and cream pots, sugar tongs and three-tiered cake stands are essential to the sense of theatre. The delicate chinaware is – of course – matching, the pattern on the cups

'Afternoon Tea now is a celebration of heritage elevated with a modern sensibility.'

and plates in harmony to unify the whole service. All of this creates an ambiance that feels exclusive, special, indulgent and opulent – a sense that no motif is too small; no cake fork too shiny.

The importance of service

It is, though, with our service team that the responsibility for our guests' overall experience really lies. Each member of staff is host for the day; the player on the stage of Afternoon Tea. Dressed immaculately in crisp uniforms, the servers move with confidence and well-practised grace.

Most of our guests come to Afternoon Tea at The Langham to celebrate a special occasion. At any one time, it's likely that we have more guests who are new to the experience than regulars. We know that, as special as it is to have Afternoon Tea, its lack of familiarity can feel intimidating for those who have never visited before: the menu is unusual, the tea list lengthy, and seemingly every moment is flecked with quirky traditions. The first and most important focus for our service team, then, is to ensure that not only are they knowledgeable and precise when they explain how things work, but also warm and engaging. Their role is to guide the process, to describe and unravel, to be so attuned to the progress of a table's experience that they can top-up an empty tea cup or refill a plate of scones even before the guests themselves are aware they are running low.

All these pieces of our Afternoon Tea puzzle form our signature style – the pace, the place, the table setting and the individual, unparalleled and warm and inviting care. It is style and elegance not just in the immaculately beautiful sandwiches, pastries and cakes, but in the immaculate service too.

A MENU FOR AFTERNOON TEA

Languishing between lunch and dinner in the traditional pattern of 'three meals a day', afternoon tea is a treat. For that reason alone, it must look spectacular, each element artfully arranged to match the occasion; and it must feel as indulgent as the setting promises without being overwhelming. The pastries will often nod to a theme, whether that's art, fashion or a season. Beyond London, afternoon tea must draw inspiration from the hotel's heritage combined with that of its location. Those locations infuse their own take on the experience, while remaining faithful to the legacy of the first teas, over 150 years before.

To keep the afternoon tea experience fresh and relevant, it's important to keep changing up the ingredients and menu selections as the seasons turn. In this way, the chefs not only showcase the best ingredients at the peak of their deliciousness, but also give our returning guests something new to look forward to. A summer menu will highlight the best fresh berries; in the autumn, it will call for the most delicious hazelnuts and pears. For us, it's also imperative to source the choicest ingredients from the best farmers and purveyors in the region, which we do meticulously.

While the tradition of Afternoon Tea may be British, the precise menu should speak to its location. The Langham Hotels have reinterpreted the tradition within their cities, showing respect for local preferences, ingredients and tastes. Each hotel carries the heritage and spirit of the London original but tailors its experience to suit its cultural context. In America, guests often prefer more intricate tartlets and pastries than the traditional finger sandwiches of Britain. In Asia, the teams work hard to lower the sweetness levels of the pastries and offer airier and lighter textures. These variations make the experience more relevant to each region without compromising the heritage of the tradition altogether. Ingredient selection itself also reflects regional influence. In Shanghai, the tea menu includes robust Chinese teas like aged pu'ers and fermented white teas that offer guests a taste of the country's deep tea heritage; in Jakarta, tropical fruits add vibrancy and colour to the pastries.

The Langham, Shanghai, Xintiandi. Artwork by Feng Xiao-Min

THE LANGHAM AFTERNOON TEA EXPERIENCE

A perfect afternoon tea begins with a perfect cup of tea itself (and perhaps a glass of Champagne for a particularly special celebration). A broad and varied tea menu at The Langham's Afternoon Tea is like the wine menu in a restaurant. Whether our guests are looking for a loyal favourite or to discover something new, there is a brew for everyone.

At The Langham, we always choose loose-leaf tea. Unlike tea bags, which often contain broken leaves or powdered teas, loose leaf provides whole leaves that unfurl beautifully when steeped, developing a more complex and nuanced flavour. The loose-leaf tea and its little tea strainer enhance the theatre of the tea ritual.

Understanding the teas and how to brew them to perfection is an art form. Black teas like an English Breakfast, Darjeeling or Earl Grey are best with water just off the boil and a steeping time of around 3 to 5 minutes. Green teas, such as Senchas and Long Jings, require slightly cooler water and a shorter steep to avoid bitterness. Oolong teas, white teas and herbal infusions all have their own ideal brewing conditions, too. When you're brewing at home, always check the packaging – it will give you the perfect brew times for your tea. Re-infusing the leaves in the pot with fresh hot water is essential after the first cups – the second infusion is often more nuanced, offering sweeter, less bitter notes. Of course some teas work perfectly with a splash of milk, the dairy rounding out the flavour profile. We encourage our guests to pour their own milk (always after brewing the tea), allowing them to find their perfect balance and colour.

Tea and food pairings

Pairing tea with food is as much an art as wine-pairing – and just as subjective. Each tea has its own aroma, tannin level and flavour profile and that means it might perfectly complement or unexpectedly clash with certain dishes. A light, floral tea, like a White Peony or Jasmine, pairs beautifully with lightly flavoured pastries; a raisiny, malty Assam Breakfast can stand up to the more robust savoury flavours of foods such as beef

'The experience of Afternoon Tea at The Langham is carefully crafted with every detail in mind...'

and smoked salmon. Matchas and Senchas, each with their grassy notes are good partners for fruitier pastries. Herbal teas such as chamomile, toasted buckwheat tea or rooibos offer delicious, caffeine-free alternatives. Like everything in food and dining, the aim is always for balance. The tea should lift and complement the food, not compete with it.

From first moments to last

Of course, the experience of Afternoon Tea at The Langham is carefully crafted with every detail in mind, from the minute our guests arrive to the minute they leave. Greeted with a warm smile, guests have a member of staff escort them to their table. Here, they are presented with their menus and the opportunity for any explanations they might need. Before leaving the guests to study the menu, a server will offer of a glass of Champagne or sparkling wine, ahead of the arrival of cups of tea themselves.

Finely attuned to the subtlest hint that a table is ready, a server will arrive to take the order and serve the tea. Then begins the time-honoured sequence of courses, each with friendly explanation if needed, and arriving perfectly timed. First come the sandwiches, with tasting notes on the fillings and types of bread. Once the sandwiches are eaten, our server will clear the table, refresh the tea and re-set the cutlery ready for pastries and scones. Guests are invited to choose a new tea for their sweet courses.

Out come the pastries, perfect in every detail; then the scones on two-tier stands, with scones on top and jams and clotted cream below. Finally come the sharing cakes – delicate mouthfuls for everyone to taste. Of course, we understand that, by then, palates may be satisfied and stomachs full, at which point we will happily box any remaining cakes for our guests to take away... perhaps as an impending midnight snack or a treat for elevenses the following day, but always to remind them of their afternoon in our cherished and impeccable care.

The Langham, London

TEA PAIRING

The Langham Afternoon Tea is an experience that goes beyond exquisite sandwiches, cakes and pastries; it's also about finding the perfect tea to accompany them. Each tea is carefully chosen to enhance the character of the food in subtle, delicious ways. These lists explore each main category of tea, identifying the dominant characteristics that inspire our suggested recipe pairings.

BLACK TEA

Bold, malty, tannic; sometimes with notes of dried fruit or spice

—

Stronger, umami-forward flavours; smoky and rich

Aged Westcombe Cheddar with Piccalilli (p.38)

Farmhouse Egg and Cress (p.40)

Honey Roast Ham with Sauce Albert (p.50)

Roast Beef, Caramelised Onions, Stilton (p.53)

Smoked Turkey with Cranberry Stuffing (p.61)

Potato Farls with Spiced Mayo and Pickled Eggs (p.62)

—

Rich, creamy and savoury desserts; classic pastries with butter and caramel

Tonka, Fig and Blackberry Cakes (p.69)

Red Velvet Cakes (p.83)

Custard Creams (p.102)

Bread and Butter (p.117)

Vanilla Cheesecake (p.138)

Mince Pies (p.144)

Chocolate Mousse in a Glass (p.150)

GREEN TEA

Grassy, slightly bitter, vegetal, fresh

—

Creamy, fresh or herby flavours; cuts through richness

Classic Cucumber and Clotted Cream (p.34)

Roasted Courgette with Pesto Dressing (p.57)

—

Delicate pastries that benefit from a contrast with grassy notes

Raspberry and Jasmine Cake Rolls (p.75)

Matcha and Apricot Cakes (p.79)

Strawberry Pink Peppercorn Tarts (p.105)

Lemon Meringue (p.147)

Continues overleaf

OOLONG TEA

Floral, toasty, sometimes creamy or fruity; sits between green and black tea

Smoked fish and meat; good bridge for savoury and sweet-spicy flavours

Cajun-spiced Roast Chicken with Apricot Harissa (p.37)

Classic Coronation Chicken (p.42)

Hot Smoked Salmon with Dill Pickle (p.48)

Scottish Smoked Salmon with Watercress and Horseradish (p.58)

Tropical, fruity, nuts, stone fruits

Vanilla and Salted Caramel Millefeuille (p.85)

Pink Guava and Plum Cakes (p.97)

Praline Paris-Brest (p.121)

Pink Guava St. Honoré (p.131)

Caraïbe Tea Cake (p.140)

WHITE TEA

Delicate, floral, slightly sweet, airy

Soft and floral, complements goat's cheese, roots and garden-fresh flavours

Heritage Carrot Slaw with Nasturtium (p.47)

Roasted Golden Beetroot, Goat's Curd, Lamb's Lettuce (p.54)

Light, subtle flavours; almond; light sponges

Matcha and Apricot Cakes (p.79)

Pistachio and Raspberry Flowers (p.93)

Decidedly Madeleine (p.114)

Bread and Butter (p.117)

The Langham Pink Battenberg (p.127)

HERBAL TEA

Floral, citrusy, minty, spiced

Unconventional, earthy, or bitter-savoury pairings

Roast Cauliflower with Gentleman's Relish (p.44)

Flavours that benefit from an aromatic lift

Rose and Lychee Babas (p.111)

Honey Cake (p.134)

CUSTARD

AFTERNOON TEA AT HOME

The recipes in this book, all of them impressive and befitting of afternoon tea, range from some of the most decadent and intricate among those we serve at The Langham to some of the most achievable. We hope that, as you leaf through, you'll find plenty of favourites within your knowledge and skill level to be able to re-create a special occasion at home. At the end of the book, Chapter 6 (Basics) captures some of the key building blocks of perfect pâtisserie (some of which appear in some form in other recipes in the book) for you to experiment with your own creations, too.

When making afternoon tea, begin with the sandwiches, choosing just two or three options that appeal to you. One fish, one meat and one vegetarian is a good place to start. When it comes to the small and sharing cakes, look for those that are achievable in terms of composition, even if the precision will take practice. Draw inspiration from what you see, and don't assume that every element of a recipe is out of your reach – often several constituent parts of our recipes are there to give inspiration to the home cook, enabling you to learn and build as you go. That said, every chapter has simpler recipes, as well as more elaborate ones.

If you're just getting started, you might choose from some of the more recognisable key elements of a perfect afternoon tea: the sandwiches, then a round of Langham scones with cream and jam, and a beautiful selection of biscuits. If you're a seasoned baker, you may stretch your skills and add a little cake and a sharing cake, too. Remember, also, that it's the ambience – the environment, the music, the serving, the table setting – that makes our teas so special, almost as much as the cakes and other treats themselves.

You'll notice throughout the recipes that the 'makes' numbers at times seem substantial. At The Langham, each treat is often intended to be a glorious morsel – the cakes, biscuits and pastries are small and bursting with flavour, each an exquisite taste to light up the palate before moving on to the next. Their diminutive size is part of the intricate artistry that goes into their creation. With their size in mind, although we can adapt our recipe quantities to a certain extent, making elements in tiny volumes, to serve just four or six people, can be challenging. So, in the book we've tried to keep the quantities sensible and encourage you to use your freezer as much as you need. Most elements will store that way, so even if you don't use all your creations at once, in many cases you can keep them frozen to defrost for another time (and an even easier afternoon tea).

Special moulds and cutters are usually straightforward to source online, and many are used in several recipes, so – as your confidence grows – they are very much worth the investment. The same goes for specialist ingredients; although wherever suitable, we've made suggestions for more homespun alternatives that you can easily find for cooking at home.

And then there's the ceremony of the tea itself. Choose a good-quality loose-leaf option for your pot, just as we do at the hotel. Find some delicate tea cups and saucers for serving, and a beautiful milk jug for your guests to pour from themselves. With just these details, you already have the foundations of your own Afternoon Tea at The Langham.

Above all, timing is everything. Prepare as much as you can in advance, allowing you to bring your tea experience together with ease. Warm the scones just before serving and have pots of hot water ready for topping up cups of tea. Some music and fresh flowers are the finishing touches of a Langham Tea atmosphere.

CHAPTER ONE

SANDWICHES

CLASSIC CUCUMBER AND CLOTTED CREAM

MAKES 12 PORTIONS

125g clotted cream
50g cream cheese
1 tablespoon finely chopped chives
½ cucumber
8 slices of soft white bread
salt and finely ground white pepper

The Langham's sandwiches are equal parts precision, tradition and artistry. We cut to exact dimensions so that the sandwiches present well, and we choose fillings that balance the tradition of the tea with a nod to interest and contemporary tastes. The classic cucumber sandwich is a staple of the Afternoon Tea menu, but it is not easy to get right. This one pairs the cucumber with clotted cream for additional indulgence; the key is the proper seasoning of the peeled cucumbers.

In a bowl mix the clotted cream and cream cheese together. Add the chives, stir to combine, and season to taste with salt and pepper. Set aside.

Peel the cucumber and cut it in half lengthways. Using a teaspoon or melon baller, scoop out the seeds and discard them. Cut the cucumber halves along their length into thin, half-moon slices.

To assemble
Lay out the bread slices on your work surface. Divide the clotted-cream mixture equally between all of the bread slices, spreading it out in an even layer. Arrange the cucumber on top of four of the slices and season with salt and pepper. Carefully turn over the remaining bread to sandwich the filling. Cover the sandwiches, then refrigerate them for 30 minutes.

Slice off the crusts and cut each sandwich into three 3cm x 9cm finger-size portions to serve.

CAJUN-SPICED ROAST CHICKEN WITH APRICOT HARISSA

MAKES 12 PORTIONS

80g Chinese cabbage, shredded
10g apricot harissa
25g tomato passata
200g mayonnaise (see page 193), plus 30g for spreading
a pinch of Cajun spice
a pinch of cumin powder
2 teaspoons finely chopped curly parsley leaves
2 boneless chicken breasts, roasted and skinned
8 slices of harissa bread or wholegrain bread
salt and freshly ground black pepper

Blanch the shredded Chinese cabbage in boiling water for 10 seconds, then drain it and leave it to dry on kitchen paper.

In a bowl, combine the harissa, the tomato passata, the 200g of mayonnaise, and both spices. Add the parsley and stir to evenly combine.

Cut the roast chicken into 1cm dice. Add the chicken to the bowl with the mayonnaise mixture, season with salt and pepper and mix to combine.

To assemble
Lay out the bread slices on your work surface and spread them all equally using the 30g of mayonnaise. Spread the chicken mixture evenly over half of the bread slices, followed by the shredded Chinese cabbage. Carefully turn over the remaining bread to sandwich the filling. Cover the sandwiches, then refrigerate them for 30 minutes.

Slice off the crusts and cut each sandwich into three 3cm x 9cm finger-size portions to serve.

AGED WESTCOMBE CHEDDAR WITH PICCALILLI

MAKES 12 PORTIONS

- 125g Westcombe Cheddar, grated
- 125g crème fraîche
- 8 slices of brioche or wholemeal bread
- 3 tablespoons piccalilli
- 1 small bunch of watercress, leaves picked

Westcombe Cheddar, from Somerset, is mellow and deeply savoury, and its richness is balanced here by the tart piccalilli. This cheese is a true hero of the British Farming story, but you could substitute another robustly flavoured cheese, if you prefer.

In a bowl, mix the grated Cheddar and crème fraîche together until they are evenly combined.

To assemble
Lay out 4 bread slices on your work surface. Divide the piccalilli equally between all of the slices, spreading it out evenly. Then, spread the cheese mixture on top in an even layer. Arrange the watercress equally on top of each filling, then sandwich with the remaining bread. Cover the sandwiches, then refrigerate them for 30 minutes.

Slice off the crusts and cut each sandwich into three 3cm x 9cm finger-size portions to serve.

FARMHOUSE EGG AND CRESS

MAKES 8–12 PORTIONS

6 free-range eggs
100g mayonnaise (see page 193), plus 30g for spreading
20g Dijon mustard
1 tablespoon snipped chives, plus optional extra to garnish
8 slices of soft white bread or 8 small brioche rolls
2 tablespoons picked mustard cress
salt and finely ground white pepper

The quality of the mayonnaise and of the eggs are key to the success of this sandwich: use homemade mayonnaise and buy the best eggs you can find, from free-range chickens and with a rich flavour and deeply coloured yolk.

Bring a small saucepan of water to a boil, add the eggs and cook for 10 minutes to hard boil. Drain the eggs and chill them quickly in a bowl of iced water, replacing the cold water as needed.

Once the eggs are completely cold, peel them, discarding the shells. Coarsely grate the eggs into a mixing bowl. Add the 100g of mayonnaise, along with the mustard and chives, then season with salt and pepper and gently fold the mixture together to combine.

To assemble
Lay out the bread slices on your work surface and spread them all equally, using the 30g of mayonnaise. Spread the egg mixture equally over each slice, then scatter the mustard cress equally over the top on half of the slices.

Carefully turn over each cress-less slice to sandwich the others neatly. Cover the sandwiches, then refrigerate them for 30 minutes.

Slice off the crusts and cut each sandwich into three 3cm x 9cm finger-size portions to serve.

If you're using small brioche rolls, hollow out the centre of each roll and fill it with the egg mixture. Scatter over the mustard cress, and a few extra snipped chives if you wish.

CLASSIC CORONATION CHICKEN

MAKES 12 PORTIONS

1 banana shallot, peeled and very thinly sliced
1 teaspoon cornflour
50ml vegetable oil
40g mango chutney
200g mayonnaise (see page 193), plus 30g for spreading
10g mild curry powder
1 teaspoon Cajun spice
50g golden raisins
1 tablespoon finely chopped coriander leaves
2 boneless chicken breasts, roasted and skinned
8 slices of harissa bread or wholemeal bread
50g lamb's lettuce, leaves picked
salt and freshly ground black pepper

So much has been said about this filling, created to celebrate the coronation of Queen Elizabeth II in 1953, and it is loved with good reason. Lightly spiced and richly flavoured, with added acidity from the golden raisins, like the then Queen herself, it has perfect balance and poise.

Tip the shallot slices into a bowl and sprinkle over the cornflour. Toss to coat, then shake off the excess flour.

Heat the oil in a small frying pan over a medium heat. Add the dusted shallots and fry for 3–4 minutes, turning occasionally, until golden brown and crispy. Remove the shallots from the pan and leave them to drain and cool on kitchen paper.

In a bowl, combine the mango chutney, the 200g of mayonnaise, and the curry powder, Cajun spice, raisins, coriander leaves and shallots and season to taste.

Cut the roasted chicken into 1cm dice. Add the chicken to the bowl with the mayonnaise mixture and mix everything together to evenly combine.

To assemble

Lay out the bread slices on your work surface and spread them all equally using the 30g of mayonnaise.

Equally top half of the slices with the coronation chicken mixture, spreading it out in an even layer. Arrange the picked lamb's lettuce on top of the chicken. Carefully turn over the other bread slices to sandwich the filling. Cover the sandwiches, then refrigerate them for 30 minutes.

Slice off the crusts and cut each sandwich into three 3cm x 9cm finger-size portions to serve.

ROAST CAULIFLOWER WITH GENTLEMAN'S RELISH

MAKES 12 PORTIONS

200g cauliflower
50g unsalted butter, softened
12g anchovies
a pinch of finely ground white pepper
a pinch of grated nutmeg
a pinch of ground cinnamon
a pinch of mace
10g lemon juice
200g crème fraîche
8 slices of wholemeal or brioche bread
50g lamb's lettuce, trimmed
salt and freshly ground black pepper

Heat the oven to 180°C fan.

Coarsely grate the cauliflower and season it with salt and pepper. Tip the grated cauliflower into a roasting tin and roast for about 10 minutes, until golden brown. Leave to cool, then cover and chill until needed (up to 2 days).

To make the gentleman's relish combine the butter, anchovies, spices and lemon juice in a blender or food processor and mix until smooth. Scoop the mixture into a bowl and fold in the crème fraîche and cooled roasted cauliflower to evenly combine.

To assemble
Lay out the bread slices on your work surface. Spread the gentleman's relish equally over the top of all of the slices, then top half of the slices with the lamb's lettuce. Carefully turn over the other bread slices to sandwich the filling. Cover the sandwiches, then refrigerate them for 30 minutes.

Slice off the crusts and cut each sandwich into three 3cm x 9cm finger-size portions to serve.

HERITAGE CARROT SLAW WITH NASTURTIUM

MAKES 12 PORTIONS

- 300g heritage carrots, peeled and grated (use coloured carrots, if available)
- a pinch of ground cardamom
- 50g clotted cream
- 100g crème fraîche
- 20g nasturtium leaves, finely sliced
- 8 slices of masala bread or sourdough
- salt and freshly ground black pepper

This is a modern sandwich that leans into the plant world for heft. The striking, peppery nasturtium leaves provide a counterpoint for the beautifully coloured sweet carrots. The result is perfect harmony.

In a colander, mix the grated carrots with a good pinch of salt and the ground cardamom and set the colander over a bowl. Leave the carrots to soften for 2 hours to draw out any excess moisture.

In a bowl, combine the clotted cream, crème fraîche, drained carrots and the nasturtium leaves and season the mixture with salt and pepper.

To assemble
Lay out the bread slices on your work surface. Divide the slaw equally between half of the bread slices, patting it out in an even layer. Sandwich with the remaining bread slices, then cover the sandwiches and refrigerate them for 30 minutes.

Slice off the crusts and cut each sandwich into three 3cm x 9cm finger-size portions to serve.

HOT SMOKED SALMON WITH DILL PICKLE

MAKES 8–12 PORTIONS

100g cream cheese
75g crème fraîche
50g Scottish smoked salmon
50g hot smoked salmon
2 teaspoons lemon juice
1 small bunch of dill, tender fronds picked and finely chopped
25g gherkin, finely diced
1 tablespoon gherkin pickle juice
8 slices of brown bread or 8 small brioche rolls
a small bunch of lamb's lettuce, leaves picked
salt and freshly ground black pepper
tiny sprigs of flat-leaf parsley, to garnish (optional)

Smoked Salmon has a long association with finger sandwiches, but in this version the salmon is hot smoked, which gives the sandwich a rich texture, and balances the sweet acidity of the dill pickles.

Pulse the cream cheese, crème fraîche, smoked salmon, hot smoked salmon and lemon juice in a food processor until all the ingredients are well combined.

Scoop the mixture into a bowl and add the dill, gherkin and pickle juice. Mix to evenly combine and season to taste.

To assemble
Lay out the bread slices on your work surface. Divide the salmon mixture equally between all of the slices, spreading it out into an even layer. Place the picked lamb's lettuce on top of half of the slices, then carefully turn over the remaining bread to sandwich the filling. Cover the sandwiches, then refrigerate them for 30 minutes.

Slice off the crusts and cut each sandwich into three 3cm x 9cm finger-size portions to serve.

If you're using small brioche rolls, hollow out the centre of each roll and fill it with the salmon mixture. Garnish with a few tiny sprigs of flat-leaf parsley, if you wish.

HONEY ROAST HAM WITH SAUCE ALBERT

MAKES 12 PORTIONS

25g horseradish cream
25g Dijon mustard
100g mayonnaise (see page 193)
8 slices of granary bread
300g honey roast ham, thinly sliced
a small bunch of rocket leaves
salt and freshly ground black pepper

Sauce Albert is an underrated classic, adding a mustardy punch to the already strongly flavoured horseradish – as a team they ably cut through the richness of the honey roast ham. They would do the same job for thinly sliced cold roast beef, as an alternative, too.

For the sauce Albert, combine the horseradish cream, Dijon mustard and mayonnaise in a bowl and season to taste. Set aside.

To assemble
Lay out the bread slices on your work surface. Divide the sauce Albert equally between all of the slices, spreading it out into an even layer. Top half of the slices with the thinly sliced ham and divide the rocket leaves equally on top of the ham. Carefully turn over the remaining bread to sandwich the filling. Cover the sandwiches, then refrigerate them for 30 minutes.

Slice off the crusts and cut each sandwich into three 3cm x 9cm finger-size portions to serve.

ROAST BEEF, CARAMELISED ONIONS, STILTON

MAKES 12 PORTIONS

2 white onions, thinly sliced
1 tablespoon canola oil
25g stilton, crumbled
100g cream cheese
8 slices of white bread
30g mayonnaise (see page 193)
300g rare roast beef, sliced wafer-thin
a small bunch of watercress, leaves picked
salt and freshly ground black pepper

Tip the onion slices into a saucepan with a splash of water and a pinch of salt. Set the pan over a low–medium heat and, once the water has evaporated, add the oil. Gently cook the onions, stirring often, for 10–15 minutes, until they are golden and caramelised. Leave the onions to cool, then transfer them to a dish, cover and chill until needed (up to 3 days).

In a small bowl, mash the stilton with a fork until smooth. Add the cream cheese and onions, season with salt and pepper, and mix to form a paste.

To assemble
Lay out the bread slices on your work surface. Spread the cheese mixture equally over half of the slices and spread the mayonnaise over the remainder. Divide the sliced beef on top of the cheese and add the watercress. Carefully turn over the mayonnaise-topped slices to sandwich the filling. Cover the sandwiches, then refrigerate them for 30 minutes.

Slice off the crusts and cut each sandwich into three 3cm x 9cm finger-size portions to serve.

ROASTED GOLDEN BEETROOT, GOAT'S CURD, LAMB'S LETTUCE

MAKES 12 PORTIONS

500g golden beetroots
2 teaspoons olive oil
15g clear honey
1 lemon thyme sprig, leaves picked
lemon juice, to taste
200g goat's curd
8 slices of harissa bread or wholemeal bread
30g mayonnaise (see page 193)
a small bunch of lamb's lettuce, leaves picked
salt and freshly ground black pepper

Heat the oven to 180°C fan.

Place the golden beetroots into a small roasting tin, drizzle with the oil, season with salt and pepper and roast for about 30 minutes, until tender. Leave the beetroots to cool, then peel them and coarsely grate the flesh.

Mix the grated beetroot with the honey, thyme leaves and a touch of lemon juice, and season to taste.

Season the goat's curd with salt and black pepper to taste.

To assemble
Lay out the bread slices on your work surface. Divide the mayo equally between half the slices and the goat's curd equally between the remainder, spreading them out into an even layer. Arrange the beetroot on top of the curd slices and top that with the lamb's lettuce. Carefully turn over the mayo-spread bread slices to sandwich the filling. Cover the sandwiches, then chill them for 30 minutes.

Slice off the crusts and cut each sandwich into three 3cm x 9cm finger-size portions to serve.

ROASTED COURGETTE WITH PESTO DRESSING

MAKES 12 PORTIONS

300g courgettes, sliced into 1cm-thick rounds
60ml olive oil
a bunch of basil, leaves picked
25g parmesan, grated, plus extra to serve
1 small garlic clove
50g cream cheese
50g soured cream
8 slices of sliced brioche or soft white bread
30g mayonnaise (see page 193)
a small bunch of rocket
salt and freshly ground black pepper

Heat the grill to medium–high.

Place the courgette slices in a single layer in a baking tray, spreading them out evenly and making sure they are flat. Brush them with a little of the oil, then grill on one side only for 2–3 minutes, until soft and golden. Cool, then cover the slices and chill until needed (up to 3 days).

In a food processor blend the basil, parmesan, garlic and remaining olive oil until the mixture resembles a pesto. Scoop the mixture into a bowl, add the cream cheese and soured cream, mix to combine and season to taste with salt and freshly ground black pepper.

To assemble
Lay out the bread slices on your work surface. Spread the pesto mixture equally over half of the slices and the mayo equally over the remainder, spreading them out into an even layer. Arrange the grilled courgette over the pesto slices and top that with equal amounts of the rocket leaves. Scatter with a little parmesan. Carefully turn over the mayo-spread bread slices to sandwich the filling. Cover the sandwiches and chill them for 30 minutes.

Slice off the crusts and cut each sandwich into three 3cm x 9cm finger-size portions to serve.

SCOTTISH SMOKED SALMON WITH WATERCRESS AND HORSERADISH

MAKES 12 PORTIONS

- 100g soured cream
- 50g clotted cream
- 50g horseradish cream
- 20g mayonnaise (see page 193)
- finely grated zest of ¼ unwaxed lemon
- 1 tablespoon brined Lilliput capers, rinsed
- 8 slices of wholegrain bread
- 300g Scottish smoked salmon slices
- a small bunch of watercress, leaves picked

The key to this all-time favourite is the quality of the smoked salmon. Look for something sustainably sourced, delicately smoked and thinly sliced.

In a bowl, mix together the soured cream, clotted cream, horseradish cream, mayonnaise, lemon zest and capers until evenly combined.

To assemble

Lay out the bread slices on your work surface. Spread the horseradish mixture equally over all of the slices. Divide the smoked salmon equally between half of the slices and top the salmon with the watercress. Carefully turn over the remaining spread bread to sandwich the filling. Cover the sandwiches, then refrigerate them for 30 minutes.

Slice off the crusts and cut each sandwich into three 3cm x 9cm finger-size portions to serve.

SMOKED TURKEY WITH CRANBERRY STUFFING

MAKES 12 PORTIONS

- 20g dried cranberries
- hot water, for soaking
- 100g sausagemeat
- 75g panko breadcrumbs
- 1 teaspoon finely chopped sage leaves
- 1 teaspoon finely chopped flat-leaf parsley leaves
- 100g carrots, julienned
- 100g savoy cabbage, julienned
- 100g mayonnaise (see page 193)
- 8 slices of white bread or wholegrain bread
- 165g smoked turkey breast, thinly sliced
- salt and freshly ground black pepper

We serve this filling seasonally, at Christmas, when it is always our guests' most requested 'top-up' sandwich. It is also the first to disappear in the kitchen when the Afternoon Tea service is over.

Soak the dried cranberries in hot water for 1 hour to soften. Drain, then pat the rehydrated berries dry with kitchen paper.

Heat the oven to 180°C fan.

In a bowl, mix together the sausagemeat, cranberries, breadcrumbs, sage and parsley. Season with salt and pepper. Line a small ovenproof dish with baking paper and tip in the sausagemeat mixture. Spread it out to an even layer and bake for about 30 minutes, or until the stuffing reaches an internal temperature of 75°C and is cooked (timing will depend on the size of your dish). Leave the stuffing to cool, then cover it and chill until needed (up to 3 days).

Lightly salt the carrots and cabbage and leave them to drain in a colander for 2 hours to remove the excess moisture.

Mix the drained vegetables with 50g of the mayonnaise.

Turn out the sausagemeat stuffing and cut it into wafer-thin slices.

To assemble

Lay out the bread slices on your work surface. Spread the remaining mayonnaise over all of the slices. Layer the sliced turkey and sausagemeat on half of the slices and top with equal amounts of the carrot slaw. Carefully turn over the remaining bread slices to sandwich the filling. Cover the sandwiches, then chill them for 30 minutes.

Slice off the crusts and cut each sandwich into three 3cm x 9cm finger-size portions to serve.

POTATO FARLS WITH SPICED MAYO AND PICKLED EGGS

MAKES 24 PORTIONS

For the potato farls
2 large baking potatoes
10g unsalted butter, softened
75g plain flour
a pinch of salt
4 tablespoons sunflower oil

For the spiced mayonnaise
1 egg yolk
1 teaspoon Dijon mustard
1 teaspoon Henderson's Relish
a few drops of Tabasco
a pinch of caster sugar
a pinch of sweet paprika
130ml sunflower oil
1 teaspoon lemon juice
salt and freshly ground black pepper

For the pickled eggs
12 quail eggs
400ml malt vinegar
finely chopped chives, to garnish

This afternoon canapé speaks to the unique heritage of The Langham's Afternoon Tea, using the time-honoured potato farl (a savoury scone or pancake) as its base.

To begin the potato farls
Heat the oven to 180°C fan. Bake the potatoes for about 1 hour, or until soft. Remove them from the oven (leave the oven on, but reduce the temperature to 150°C fan). When the potatoes are cool enough to handle, cut them in half and scoop the soft insides into a potato ricer. Press the flesh through the ricer into a bowl.

Weigh 250g of the mashed potato into a separate bowl. Add the butter, flour and pinch of salt and mix to combine.

Line a small baking tray with baking paper. Spread the potato mixture evenly into the tray to a depth of 2cm, then bake for 40 minutes, until firm and golden. Cool, then cover, and chill until needed (up to 3 days).

To make the spiced mayonnaise
Combine the egg yolk, mustard, relish, Tabasco, sugar and paprika in a bowl and whisk for 1 minute until smooth. Whisking continuously, add the oil slowly and gradually, until you have used it all and the mixture is smooth and combined. Add the lemon juice and season to taste. Cover and chill until needed (up to 3 days).

To make the pickled eggs
Prepare a bowl of iced water. Cook the quail eggs in boiling water for 2 minutes and 15 seconds, then remove them from the pan and add them to the iced water – this stops them cooking and cools them quickly.

Once the eggs are cold, pour the vinegar into a bowl and add the eggs, ensuring they are submerged. Leave them like that for 1 hour, or until the shells are soft enough to peel away easily. Peel and rinse the eggs. They will keep in an airtight container in the fridge for up to 3 days.

To finish the farls and assemble
Using a 3cm ring cutter, stamp out 24 discs from the potato mixture.

Heat the 4 tablespoons of oil in a frying pan over a medium heat. When hot, in batches, fry the potato discs on both sides (about 2 minutes per side) until golden. Alternatively, deep-fry them in oil heated to 180°C, for about 3 minutes, until golden. Set aside each batch to drain on kitchen paper while you fry the remainder, keeping the discs warm in a low oven.

To serve, top each warm farl with ½–1 teaspoon of the mayonnaise and finish with half a quail egg. Scatter with finely chopped chives, to garnish

CHAPTER TWO

LITTLE CAKES

TONKA, FIG AND BLACKBERRY CAKES

MAKES 30

For the fig Chantilly
4 fig leaves
500g 35%-fat cream or whipping cream, plus extra if needed
30g gelatine mass (see page 207)
75g 33% white chocolate (such as Valrhona Opalys), chopped

For the fig and blackberry mixture
15g caster sugar
2g pectin NH
110g fig purée
100g blackberry purée
seeds from ½ vanilla bean
20g gelatine mass (see page 207)
60g figs
40g frozen wild blueberries, defrosted

For the açai berry sweet-paste shortbread
90g unsalted butter, softened
25g icing sugar, sifted
12g egg, lightly beaten
80g T55 or plain flour
25g ground almonds
10g açai powder
2g baking powder

An afternoon-tea cake should captivate at first sight. In this case, varied piping creates an intricate design, while a light velvet spray adds texture. The flavour, full of fresh, sweet and tangy fruit, is an equal match for its beauty: fig leaves lend earthy brightness, blackberries provide a touch of tartness, and fresh figs are the crowning glory.

To make the fig Chantilly
The day before assembling the cakes, mix the fig leaves and half of the cream in a bowl. Cover and refrigerate overnight.

The next day, bring the fig cream (including the leaves) to a boil in a small saucepan over a low–medium heat. Immediately remove the pan from the heat, cover with cling film and leave to infuse for 15 minutes.

Weigh a clean pan and make a note of the weight. Strain the cream into it, work out the weight of the cream alone and add more cream to return the weight to 250g if needed. Reheat the cream to 60°C.

Remove the pan from the heat and add the gelatine mass and white chocolate. Use a stick blender to make a perfect emulsion. Add the remaining cream, mix to combine and chill until needed.

To make the fig and blackberry mixture
In a small bowl mix together the caster sugar and pectin and set aside.

In a small saucepan, combine the fig and blackberry purées and vanilla seeds and warm the mixture over a low–medium heat to 40°C. Add the pectin and sugar mixture, whisk to combine, then bring to a boil.

Remove the pan from the heat, add the gelatine mass and mix to melt so that the mixture is smooth and evenly combined. Leave to cool, then refrigerate to set.

Once set, use a hand blender to blitz the mixture until smooth.

Carefully peel the skin from the 60g of figs, cut the flesh into fine dice and add the dice to the purée. Add the wild blueberries, then spoon the mixture into the mini stone moulds until each is half full. Cover and refrigerate for at least 2–3 hours until set.

Continues overleaf

TONKA, FIG AND BLACKBERRY CAKES *CONTINUED*

For the tonka sponge
125g egg yolks
13g clear honey
120g egg whites
60g caster sugar
10g whole milk
10g unsalted butter
55g T55 or plain flour
2 pieces tonka bean, finely grated

For the almond crunch
60g 40% milk chocolate (such as Valrhona Jivara), chopped
60g almond praline
60g feuilletine

For the purple velvet spray
100g 33% white chocolate (such as Valrhona Opalys), chopped
100g cocoa butter
a pinch of fat-soluble red food-colouring powder
a pinch of fat-soluble blueberry food-colouring powder

To assemble
5–6 fresh figs, thinly sliced
micro herbs, such as red sorrel

You will also need
30 micro stone-shaped moulds: 5ml capacity
5cm round cutter
20cm x 30cm baking tray lined with baking paper
Spray gun
3cm round cutter
Piping bag fitted with a 1cm plain nozzle
30 Globe 26 moulds: 26ml capacity

To make the açai berry sweet-paste shortbread
In a small bowl, cream the butter and icing sugar until light. Add the egg and mix until thoroughly combined. Sift in the flour, almonds, açai powder and baking powder and mix again until thoroughly combined.

Shape the dough into a neat ball, flatten the ball into a disc and place it between two sheets of baking paper. Roll out the dough between the sheets until 2–3mm thick. Refrigerate for 30 minutes, until firm.

Heat the oven to 150°C fan.

Using the 5cm round cutter, stamp out 30 discs from the chilled dough and place them on a lined baking sheet (or silicone air mat). Bake for about 15 minutes, until crisp.

To make the tonka sponge
Heat the oven to 170°C fan.

Place the egg yolks and honey in a heatproof bowl set over a pan of barely simmering water. With a balloon whisk, whisk continuously until the mixture is pale, trebles in volume and holds a firm ribbon trail when you lift the whisk. Remove the bowl from the heat.

In another bowl, whisk the egg whites and sugar together until the mixture forms a glossy meringue.

In a small bowl in the microwave, heat the milk and butter until the milk is warm and the butter has melted.

Using a large metal spoon, fold the meringue mixture into the egg yolks. Sift in the flour and fold it in, then fold in the tonka bean until no dry patches remain.

Add 2–3 tablespoons of the cake mixture to the milk and butter mixture and mix until combined. Fold this into the main bowl of cake mixture.

Carefully spoon the cake mixture into the lined baking tray, spread it level and bake for 8–10 minutes, until the sponge has set. Leave to cool.

To make the almond crunch
Melt the milk chocolate in a bowl set over a pan of barely simmering water until it reaches 40°C. Stir the chocolate until smooth, then remove the bowl from the heat. Add the almond praline and mix using a spatula until fully combined.

Add the feuilletine, mix well and spread the mixture on to the cooled tonka sponge in a neat, even layer. Leave to cool and set.

Continues overleaf

TONKA, FIG AND BLACKBERRY CAKES *CONTINUED*

To make the purple velvet spray
In a heatproof bowl set over a pan of barely simmering water, melt the chocolate and cocoa butter together and mix until smooth. Remove the bowl from the heat, add the food colourings and, using a hand blender, blitz the mixture until smooth. Use the mixture to fill the spray gun.

To assemble
Using the 3cm round cutter, cut the almond crunch-topped cake into 30 discs.

Whip the fig Chantilly to firm peaks. Spoon the Chantilly into the piping bag fitted with a 1cm nozzle and pipe the cream into the globe moulds to half fill. Pop the fig and blackberry out of their moulds and place one on top of each portion of piped Chantilly. Pipe another layer of Chantilly over the top, then press a disc of the tonka bean cake into the cream. Cover and freeze for about 2 hours, or until solid.

Remove the cakes from the moulds and pipe more fig Chantilly on the outside of each frozen cake to coat. Spray the frozen cakes with purple velvet and refrigerate until defrosted.

To serve, place the cakes on the açai shortbreads and decorate with thinly sliced fresh figs and edible micro herbs.

RASPBERRY AND JASMINE CAKE ROLLS

MAKES 28

For the jasmine mahalbia
335g whole milk
100g 35%-fat cream or whipping cream
40g dried jasmine flowers or buds
20g light brown soft sugar
40g cornflour

For the raspberry whipped ganache
110g raspberry purée
15g liquid glucose
150g 35% white chocolate (such as Valrhona Ivoire), chopped
250g 35%-fat cream or whipping cream

For the sponge
155g whole eggs
40g egg yolks
130g caster sugar
75g egg whites
15g whole milk
15g unsalted butter
30g T55 or plain flour
20g cornflour
a few drops of red food-colouring gel or paste

For the raspberry confit (or see note in method)
285g raspberry purée
30g caster sugar
4g pectin NH
1 teaspoon lemon juice

To make the jasmine mahalbia
The night before assembling the cakes, infuse the cold milk and the cold cream in separate bowls with the jasmine, adding 30g of the jasmine to the milk and 10g to the cream. Cover and chill until needed.

The next day, in a small bowl, mix the sugar and cornflour together. Strain the jasmine-infused milk into a small saucepan, add the sugar and cornflour mixture and place the pan over a low–medium heat. Bring to a boil and cook for 1 minute, stirring continuously, to cook out the cornflour.

Remove the pan from the heat, cool the mixture, then pour it into a bowl and refrigerate for about 1 hour, until cold.

Strain the cream into the cold milk mixture and, using a hand blender, blitz until smooth and combined. Chill until needed. To assemble, spoon the mahalbia into the piping bag fitted with a 5mm plain nozzle.

To make the raspberry whipped ganache
Combine the raspberry purée and glucose in a small saucepan. Place the pan over a low–medium heat and bring the mixture to a boil. Immediately remove the pan from the heat.

Add the white chocolate and mix until emulsified. Add the cream and, using a hand blender, blitz until smooth. Cover and chill overnight or until needed.

To make the sponge
Heat the oven to 170°C fan.

Place the whole eggs, yolks and 95g of the sugar in a heatproof bowl set over a pan of barely simmering water. Whisk continuously with a balloon whisk until the mixture trebles in volume, is pale and light and will hold a firm ribbon trail when you lift the whisk.

In another bowl or in a stand mixer, whisk the egg whites and remaining 35g of sugar together until the mixture holds firm peaks and is glossy.

In a small bowl, heat the milk and butter in the microwave until the milk is warm and the butter has melted.

Using a large metal spoon, fold the meringue into the eggs. Then, sift in the flour and cornflour and add the few drops of food colouring. Fold everything together until no dry patches remain and you have a good, even red colour.

Continues overleaf

To finish
28 white chocolate sticks or curls
28 raspberries

You will also need
Piping bag fitted with a 5mm plain nozzle
Two 33cm x 23cm Swiss roll tins, each lined with baking paper

Add 2–3 tablespoons of the cake mixture to the warm milk and butter and mix until combined. Tip this back into the cake mixture and fold to fully incorporate.

Carefully spoon the cake mixture equally into the lined Swiss roll tins. Spread the mixture level and bake for 8–10 minutes, until the sponge has set.

Leave to cool, then turn out the sponges on to clean baking paper. Trim the edges and cut each cake in half lengthways.

To make the raspberry confit
Combine the raspberry purée with the sugar and pectin in a small saucepan and bring to a boil over a medium heat. Immediately remove the pan from the heat. Add the lemon juice, mix to combine and leave to cool.

This makes more than you need for this recipe but it will keep in a sterilised, airtight jar in the fridge for up to 2 weeks. Alternatively, you could use 4 tablespoons of good-quality, shop-bought raspberry jam and sieve it to remove the pips.

To assemble
Spread a tablespoon of the raspberry confit on to each sponge half.

Whisk the raspberry ganache until firm and spreadable and spread this on to each sponge in an even layer. Refrigerate the sponges for 10 minutes to cool.

Remove the sponges from the fridge and, one at a time, from the long side closest to you and rolling away from your body, roll each one into a long, tight spiral roll. Wrap the rolls tightly in cling film and freeze them for 1 hour until firm.

Remove the rolls from the freezer and cut each one into equal 3–4cm lengths.

Pipe the whipped jasmine mahalbia on top of each portion and leave the cakes to defrost in the fridge. Finish with a white chocolate stick or curl and a raspberry to serve.

MATCHA AND APRICOT CAKES

MAKES ABOUT 27

For the matcha sponge
40g canola oil
10g high-quality matcha powder
60g whole milk
50g T55 or plain flour
100g egg yolks
150g egg whites
55g caster sugar
½ teaspoon lemon juice

For the matcha shortcrust pastry
155g T55 or plain flour
40g icing sugar
20g ground almonds
5g high-quality matcha powder
70g unsalted butter, cubed and chilled
30g eggs, lightly beaten

For the vanilla Chantilly
300g 35%-fat cream or whipping cream
35g caster sugar
seeds from ¼ vanilla bean
20g gelatine mass (see page 207)
60g mascarpone

For the apricot confit (or see note in method)
160g apricot purée
¼ teaspoon vanilla paste
20g caster sugar
20g glucose powder
3g pectin NH

With grassy notes that are ideal for desserts, Japanese matcha is gaining popularity among our guests. It is made using green tea leaves, and its subtle bitterness pairs beautifully with apricot jam. Super clean-cut edges always give sliced cakes an elegant finish.

To make the matcha sponge
Heat the oven to 170°C fan.

Using a balloon whisk combine the canola oil and matcha powder in a mixing bowl. Add the milk, sift in the flour and whisk until smooth and thoroughly combined. Add the egg yolks and mix until smooth.

In another mixing bowl or in a stand mixer fitted with the whisk, whisk the egg whites, sugar and lemon juice until they hold soft peaks. Using a large metal spoon, gently fold the egg whites into the matcha mixture.

Scoop the batter into the prepared baking tin, spread it level with a palette knife and bake for about 12 minutes, until the sponge is light and springy.

To make the matcha shortcrust pastry
Sift the flour, icing sugar, almonds and matcha powder into a bowl. Add the butter and rub in the cubes until the mixture has a sand-like texture. Add the eggs and mix to form a smooth dough. Roll out the dough to a rough rectangle between two sheets of baking paper until 2mm thick. Chill the dough for 30 minutes.

Meanwhile, heat the oven to 140°C fan. Line a baking sheet with baking paper (or use a silicone air mat).

Using the 4cm square cutter, stamp out squares of the pastry and place them on the lined baking sheet (or mat), then cover with another baking sheet or mat. Bake, sandwiched flat, for 15 minutes, until firm. Then, remove the top baking sheet (or mat) and leave to cool.

To make the vanilla Chantilly
In a small saucepan over a low–medium heat, warm half of the cream with the sugar and vanilla seeds until the cream reaches 60°C. Remove the pan from the heat, add the gelatine mass and stir until thoroughly melted and combined. Strain the mixture through a fine-meshed sieve into a clean bowl. Add the remaining cream and the mascarpone and use a hand blender to blitz until smooth.

Leave the Chantilly to cool, then cover and chill until needed.

Continues overleaf

MATCHA AND APRICOT CAKES *CONTINUED*

To finish
27 sugar paste or moulded chocolate butterflies (optional)
edible gold leaf (optional)

You will also need
37cm x 26cm baking tin, lined (base and sides) with baking paper
4cm square cutter
Piping bag fitted with a 1cm plain nozzle

To make the apricot confit
Combine the apricot purée and vanilla in small saucepan. In a small bowl, mix together the sugar, glucose powder and pectin NH, then sprinkle the mixture on to the apricot purée. Mix until smooth and thoroughly combined.

Place the pan over a low–medium heat and bring the mixture to a boil. Immediately pour the mixture into a clean bowl. Leave the confit to cool and set, then cover and chill until needed.

Alternatively, at home you could use good-quality, shop-bought apricot jam, blended until smooth as below.

To assemble
Turn out the cake on to a clean sheet of baking paper and peel off the lining paper. Trim the edges of the cake to neaten, then cut the sponge in half to give two long strips of roughly 12cm x 35cm.

Using a hand blender, blitz the apricot confit until smooth, then spread a thin layer of it over one strip of the matcha cake (you may not need all the confit; any leftover will keep, covered, in the fridge for up 7 days). Freeze the cakes for 15 minutes to firm up.

Whip the vanilla Chantilly until smooth and spread it to a thickness of 5mm on top of the apricot confit. Cover with the second cake layer. Spoon the remaining cream into the piping bag fitted with a 1cm plain nozzle.

Chill the cake again for 1 hour, then cut it into neat 4cm squares. Place a matcha pastry square on each side of the cake layers, sticking the squares to the cake with either a little apricot confit or Chantilly cream.

Stand the cakes on their sides and pipe a bulb of vanilla Chantilly in one corner, then decorate with a butterfly to finish. A little edible gold leaf is pretty too.

RED VELVET CAKES

MAKES 21

For the red velvet sponge
85g unsalted butter, softened
140g caster sugar
¼ teaspoon salt
70g eggs, lightly beaten
180g T55 or plain flour
5g cocoa powder
3.5g bicarbonate of soda
80g whole milk
80g fresh beetroot juice or whole milk
14g lemon juice
a few tiny drops of red food-colouring paste

For the orange cream-cheese filling
320g cream cheese, at room temperature
95g icing sugar, sifted
65g unsalted butter, melted and cooled slightly
1 teaspoon finely grated orange zest
30g orange purée or orange juice

To finish
200g Valrhona Raspberry Inspiration chocolate
½ recipe quantity vanilla Chantilly (see page 208)
21 raspberries, halved
micro herbs, such as red amaranth or sorrel

You will also need
30cm x 40cm baking tin, lined (base and sides) with baking paper
Acetate sheet
4cm square cutter
Piping bag fitted with a 5mm plain nozzle

To make the red velvet sponge
Heat the oven to 170°C fan.

Cream the butter, sugar and salt in a stand mixer fitted with the paddle on medium speed until pale, light and fluffy. Little by little, add the beaten eggs, mixing well between each addition.

Sift the flour, cocoa and bicarbonate of soda together into a jug, then add half to the cake mixture and mix on low speed to roughly incorporate.

In a jug combine the milk, beetroot juice (or additional milk) and lemon juice.

Add half the milk mixture to the cake batter, beating continuously until smooth.

Add the remaining dry ingredients to the cake batter, mixing on low to roughly incorporate, then add the remaining wet ingredients. Mix until smooth, then stir in the food colouring to an even colour. Spoon the mixture into the prepared baking tin and spread it level. Bake for 15–16 minutes, until set and risen. Leave to cool.

To make the orange cream-cheese filling
Beat the cream cheese and icing sugar together until smooth.

Add the melted butter and mix until smooth. Add the orange zest and purée or juice and mix again until thoroughly combined. Cover and chill until needed.

To finish
Turn the cake on to a clean sheet of baking paper and remove the lining paper. Trim the edges and cut the cake into three strips, each roughly 12cm x 28cm.

To assemble
Using a palette knife, spread the cream-cheese filling equally over two of the cake strips in an even layer. Neatly place one strip on top of the other, spread sides uppermost, and cover with the third cake strip so that you have a neat stack of three cake layers with two layers of filling. Cover the cake and refrigerate for 2 hours.

Using the method on page 200, temper the Raspberry Inspiration chocolate. Pour the tempered chocolate over the acetate sheet and use a palette knife to spread it out evenly until 1–2mm thick. Leave to set at room temperature. Using a 4cm square cutter, stamp out 21 squares, then cut each square into two triangles. Chill until needed.

Neatly cut the chilled cake into 4–5cm squares and stand the cakes on their sides. Using a little Chantilly, stick a chocolate triangle on either side of each cake.

Spoon the Chantilly into the piping bag fitted with a 5mm plain nozzle and pipe 6 bulbs of cream on top of each cake. Decorate each cake with two raspberry halves and micro herbs.

VANILLA AND SALTED CARAMEL MILLEFEUILLE

MAKES 30

For the inverted puff pastry
For the detrempe (base dough)
420g T55 or plain flour, plus extra for dusting
18g salt
135g unsalted butter
180g cold water
3g white vinegar
For the beurrage
180g T45 or 00 flour
450g unsalted butter

For the vanilla Chantilly
300g 35%-fat cream or whipping cream
35g caster sugar
seeds from ¼ vanilla bean
20g gelatine mass (see page 207)
60g mascarpone

For the caramel sauce (see also note in method)
190g 35%-fat cream or whipping cream
40g liquid glucose
175g caster sugar
50g unsalted butter
2g salt
25g 35% white chocolate (such as Valrhona Dulcey), chopped

To finish
icing sugar, for dusting

You will also need
Piping bag fitted with a 3–5mm plain nozzle
Piping bag fitted with an 8mm plain nozzle

This pastry barely needs an introduction; its charm lies in its flavour and the apparent simplicity of its 'one-thousand layers' (the literal translation of millefeuille). It is a classically perfect afternoon-tea treat.

To make the inverted puff pastry
To make the detrempe, place the flour, salt and butter in a stand mixer fitted with the dough hook and slowly mix everything to loosely combine. Add the cold water and vinegar and keep mixing for 3 minutes on low speed, then increase the speed to medium and mix for about 10 minutes, until the dough is smooth, elastic and will create a clear windowpane when a little of it is stretched between your fingers. Once the dough is ready, flatten it into a neat rectangle, cover and refrigerate overnight.

Meanwhile, prepare the beurrage. Combine the flour and butter in the stand mixer fitted with the paddle and mix until smooth. Transfer the mixture to a large sheet of baking paper, cover with a second sheet of paper and roll the beurrage into a neat rectangle that is of even thickness and is twice as large as the detrempe. Cover the beurrage and refrigerate overnight.

Place the beurrage on a floured work surface and place the dough on top in the middle of it. Fold the beurrage around the dough to enclose it completely. Cover and chill again for 20 minutes.

If you're rolling the pastry by hand, flour the work surface and roll the dough to a long, neat rectangle that is three times as long as it is wide. Fold the top of the rectangle down to the middle to cover the middle third and the bottom third up to cover this. This is a single fold. Cover and chill the pastry for 30 minutes.

Repeat this folding and chilling a further 4 times to make a total of 5 single folds. Then, chill the dough for 2 hours or until needed.

If you're using a dough breaker, roll out the dough to a long rectangle. In total make 5 single folds, resting the dough in the fridge for at least 1 hour between each single fold.

Once the folds are complete and the dough has rested, flour the work surface again. Cut the dough into 3 equal pieces and roll each into a neat rectangle, 3mm thick. Transfer each rectangle of dough to a lined baking sheet and refrigerate for 1 hour.

Continues overleaf

Heat the oven to 190°C fan.

Trim the edges of each puff pastry rectangle. Bake in batches: cover the first piece of raw pastry with another sheet of baking paper and place another baking sheet on top. Alternatively, place the dough between two silicone air mats. Bake the pastry for 30–35 minutes or until crisp and golden. Repeat with the remaining pastry.

To make the vanilla Chantilly
In a small saucepan over a low–medium heat, warm half of the cream with the sugar and vanilla seeds until the cream reaches 60°C. Remove the pan from the heat, add the gelatine mass and stir until thoroughly melted and combined. Strain the mixture through a fine-meshed sieve into a clean bowl. Add the remaining cream and the mascarpone and use a hand blender to blitz until smooth.

Leave the Chantilly to cool, then cover and chill it for 12 hours or overnight.

To make the caramel sauce
In a small saucepan, bring the cream and glucose to a boil over a low–medium heat, then immediately remove it from the heat.

Meanwhile, in another pan heat the sugar over a medium heat until melted (you can swirl, but don't stir). Continue to cook, without stirring, until the sugar becomes a dark caramel, swirling the pan to ensure the caramel cooks evenly.

Slide the caramel off the heat and slowly pour in the hot cream, stirring continuously to combine. Add the butter and salt, bring to a boil again and cook until the mixture reaches 112°C.

Remove the pan from the heat, add the chocolate and, using a hand blender, blitz the sauce to a perfect emulsion.

Leave the caramel to cool, then transfer it to the piping bag fitted with a 3–5mm plain nozzle. Keep the caramel at room temperature for at least 12 hours before you use it.

Alternatively, at home you could use shop-bought caramel sauce.

To assemble
Trim the baked puff pastry sheets and cut them into neat 4cm squares. You should get 90 squares altogether.

Whip the Chantilly until it holds firm peaks, then spoon it into the piping bag fitted with an 8mm nozzle. Pipe 9 bulbs on top of two thirds (30) of the pastry squares. Pipe dots of caramel sauce in between the Chantilly.

Stack two cream-topped pastry squares on top of each other and finish with a final layer of plain pastry.

Dust with icing sugar to serve.

ALMOND APRICOT CAKES

MAKES 30

For the almond sponges
180g ground almonds
180g caster sugar
265g eggs, lightly beaten
73g unsalted butter, melted
58g egg whites

For the lemon thyme oat streusel
1.5g lemon thyme leaves, chopped
5g water
1g bicarbonate of soda
30g desiccated coconut
75g T55 or plain flour
55g rolled oats
50g caster sugar
75g unsalted butter
15g golden syrup

For the almond inspiration namelaka
100g whole milk
24g gelatine mass (see page 207)
165g Valrhona Almond Inspiration chocolate
200g 35%-fat cream or whipping cream

For the apricot coulis
200g apricot purée
20g water
25g caster sugar
15g lemon purée or 3 teaspoons lemon juice
20g SOSA Gelcrem Cold

Almond tofu is a beloved Chinese dessert believed to have originated during the Han Dynasty between 206BCE and 220CE. It has a silky, creamy texture that pairs perfectly with the tartness of apricot.

To make the almond sponges
Heat the oven to 180°C fan.

Mix the ground almonds, 145g of the caster sugar and the beaten eggs in a heatproof mixing bowl. Set the bowl over a pan of barely simmering water. Do not allow the bottom of the bowl to touch the water. Whisk continuously until the mixture holds a ribbon trail when you lift the whisk, and it reaches a temperature of 40°C.

Remove the bowl from the heat, add the melted butter and fold to combine.

In another bowl, whisk the egg whites and remaining 35g of caster sugar to soft peaks. Using a large metal spoon, fold the meringue into the egg-yolk mixture until no streaks remain.

Spoon the cake into the lined Swiss roll tins and bake for 12–15 minutes, until the sponges have set.

To make the lemon thyme oat streusel
Heat the oven to 150°C fan. Line a large baking sheet with baking paper.

Combine all of the streusel ingredients in a food processor and pulse until combined.

Roll the mixture between two sheets of baking paper until 2–3mm thick and, using the 3–4cm round cutter, stamp out 30 discs. Arrange these on the lined baking sheet and bake for 18 minutes, until crisp and golden.

To make the almond inspiration namelaka
Bring the milk to a boil in a small pan over a low–medium heat. Immediately remove the pan from the heat, add the gelatine mass and mix to combine.

Partially melt the chocolate (some pieces molten, some firmer) in a heatproof bowl set over a pan of barely simmering water, then remove the bowl from the heat.

Mixing with a spatula, slowly combine the warm milk mixture with the chocolate to make a smooth emulsion. Leave to cool slightly, then add the cream and use a hand blender to blitz to a perfect emulsion. Cover and refrigerate for 12 hours.

To make the apricot coulis
Using a hand blender, combine all the coulis ingredients in a bowl. Spoon the coulis into a piping bag fitted with a 1cm plain nozzle. Set aside until needed.

Continues overleaf

ALMOND APRICOT CAKES *CONTINUED*

For the apricot confit
20g caster sugar
20g glucose powder
2.5g pectin NH
160g apricot purée
2g vanilla paste

For the white chocolate whipping ganache
170g 33% white chocolate (such as Valrhona Opalys), broken up
220g whole milk
7g potato starch
15g liquid glucose
25g gelatine mass (see page 207)
130g 35%-fat cream or whipping cream

For the tofu pudding
150g silken tofu
97g soya milk
14g almond paste (70%)
15g gelatine mass (see page 207)
30g caster sugar
10g SOSA Gelcrem Cold

For the chocolate collar
300g 33% white chocolate (such as Valrhona Opalys), broken up
a pinch of fat-soluble orange food-colouring powder

To decorate
30 edible yellow rose petals

To make the apricot confit
Combine the sugar, glucose and pectin NH in a small bowl. Add the apricot purée and vanilla and mix until smooth.

Transfer the mixture to a small saucepan, bring to a boil, then immediately remove the pan from the heat and pour the confit into a large jar or container.

Leave to cool and set, then, using a hand blender, blitz until smooth.

To make the white chocolate whipping ganache
Melt the chocolate in a heatproof bowl over a pan of barely simmering water. Stir until smooth and remove from the heat.

In a jug, mix 75g of the milk with the potato starch and set aside.

In a small saucepan, heat the rest of the milk and all the glucose over a medium–low heat, until it reaches 85°C.

Pour the potato-starch mixture into the milk-glucose mixture and bring the liquid back to a boil. Simmer for at least 30 seconds to thicken.

Remove the pan from the heat, add the gelatine mass and mix until melted and combined. Add the melted chocolate and use a hand blender to blitz to a perfect emulsion.

Pour the cream into the mixture and blend again. Cover and chill for at least 12 hours.

Before using, whisk the mixture to thicken, then spoon it into a piping bag fitted with a 1cm plain nozzle.

To make the tofu pudding
Using a hand blender, blitz together all the ingredients except the Gelcrem Cold.

In a small saucepan or in the microwave in short bursts, warm half the mixture, stirring to melt the gelatine mass. Remove from the heat and combine with the remaining mixture. Add the Gelcrem Cold and blend for 2 minutes on high speed until smooth.

Pour the pudding mixture into a piping bag fitted with a 1cm nozzle and leave to cool.

To assemble
Place one streusel disc into the bottom of each cylinder mould.

Cut the sponge into 4cm x 13cm strips and use these to line the insides of the moulds. Pipe in the tofu pudding to quarter fill the sponge, then freeze for at least 1 hour, or until firm.

Spoon the chilled namelaka into the final piping bag fitted with a 1cm plain nozzle and pipe it on top of the tofu pudding so that you fill the sponge to half full. Freeze again until firm.

You will also need
Two 30cm x 40cm Swiss roll tins, greased and lined with baking paper
3–4cm round cutter
4 piping bags, each fitted with a 1cm plain nozzle
Thirty 4cm x 4cm cylinder moulds
Piping bag fitted with a 1mm plain nozzle
30 acetate sheets, each measuring 14cm x 5cm

Spoon a layer of apricot confit on top of the namelaka to fill the moulds until three-quarters full, leaving a little gap at the top.

Pipe a bulb of apricot coulis in the middle of each cake and cover with a bulb of whipped ganache. Chill again until firm.

Meanwhile, prepare the chocolate collar.

For the chocolate collar
Melt the chocolate in a heatproof bowl over a pan of barely simmering water. Stir until smooth, remove from the heat and leave to cool slightly.

Spoon 2 tablespoons of the melted chocolate into another bowl, add a pinch of orange food-colouring powder and mix well to thoroughly combine. Spoon the mixture into the piping bag fitted with a 1mm nozzle.

Lay your acetate sheets on flat baking sheets. Pipe fine lines using the orange-coloured white chocolate over the sheets and refrigerate for 5 minutes to set.

Using an offset palette knife, spread the remaining melted chocolate into a 1–2mm-thick layer across all of the sheets over the set orange lines and leave until almost set (about 10–15 minutes).

Remove the cakes from the moulds and wrap each cake in a chocolate collar with the acetate on the outside. Chill to set firm, then carefully peel away the acetates.

Decorate each cake with a rose petal to serve.

PISTACHIO AND RASPBERRY FLOWERS

MAKES 30

For the raspberry jelly
75g raspberry purée
50g water
4g gelatine powder
12g caster sugar
125g raspberries

For the pistachio sablé
58g unsalted butter, softened
30g icing sugar
36g pistachio paste (100%)
70g egg whites
4g salt
160g T55 or plain flour, sifted
100g finely ground pistachios
4g baking powder

For the pistachio sponge
75g finely ground pistachios
95g egg yolks
110g caster sugar
115g egg whites
65g T55 or plain flour
45g unsalted butter, melted

For the light pistachio Chantilly
100g whole milk
385g 35%-fat cream or whipping cream
24g gelatine mass (see page 207)
125g 33% white chocolate (such as Valrhona Opalys), chopped
100g pistachio paste (100%)

We love the many ways in which this cake uses pistachio: kneaded into the pastry, blended into the cream, toasted for the sponge, mixed into the chocolate and finely ground for crunch. Elegance comes in the form of a glossy dome of raspberry jelly – a burst of fruit flavour as the centre of the 'flower', and a classic pairing for the nuts.

To make the raspberry jelly
In a small saucepan, mix the raspberry purée with the water. Add the gelatine, mix, and set aside for 15–20 minutes for the gelatine to bloom. Add the sugar and heat the mixture to 50°C, swirling the pan to melt evenly. Remove the pan from the heat, add the raspberries and use a hand blender on low speed to blend until smooth.

Immediately pour the mixture equally into the dome moulds, allowing 8g per mould, and freeze for 2 hours, or until solid. Pop the solid jellies out of the moulds on to a tray and return them to the freezer until needed. Clean the moulds.

To make the pistachio sablé
In a mixing bowl, beat together the butter, icing sugar and pistachio paste until smooth. Add the egg whites and salt and mix again to combine. Add the flour, pistachios and baking powder and mix again to a smooth, combined dough.

Roll out the dough between two sheets of baking paper until 2mm thick, then refrigerate for 20 minutes.

Using the 6–7cm round cutter, stamp out 30 discs from the sablé. Use these to line the dome moulds or bun tins. Chill for 20 minutes while you heat the oven to 145°C fan. Then, place the moulds in the oven and bake the sablé for about 15 minutes, until crisp. Leave to cool, then remove the sablés from the moulds and set aside.

To make the pistachio sponge
Heat the oven to 150°C fan. Tip the ground pistachios on to a baking tray and roast them for about 12 minutes, until toasted. Leave to cool. Meanwhile, increase the oven temperature to 170°C fan.

Using a stand mixer fitted with a whisk, beat the egg yolks with 65g of the sugar until they are thick, pale and hold a ribbon trail.

In another bowl, whisk the egg whites until they hold soft peaks. Whisking continuously, gradually add the remaining 45g of caster sugar until the mixture is glossy and holds soft peaks.

Continues overleaf

PISTACHIO AND RASPBERRY FLOWERS *CONTINUED*

For the raspberry gel
200g raspberry purée
15g lemon purée or 3 teaspoons lemon juice
25g caster sugar
12.5g SOSA Gelcrem Cold
25g water

For the pistachio chocolate
130g 33% white chocolate (such as Valrhona Opalys), broken up
100g pistachio paste (100%)
50g very finely ground pistachios

For the chocolate flowers
100g 33% white chocolate (such as Valrhona Opalys), broken up
a pinch of fat-soluble green food-colouring powder

To finish
½ quantity neutral glaze, warmed to 34°C (see page 202)

You will also need
Thirty 4cm ovensafe dome moulds or bun tins
6–7cm round cutter
37cm x 26cm baking tin, lined (base and sides) with baking paper
3cm round cutter
Piping bag fitted with a 1.8cm plain nozzle
Sheet of acetate
5cm flower cutter

Using a large metal spoon, fold one third of the egg whites into the egg yolks until no streaks remain, taking care not to over-mix.

Sift the toasted pistachios and the flour into the bowl with the eggs and fold until nearly incorporated. Fold in the remaining beaten whites and, finally, the melted butter.

Spoon the mixture into the lined baking tin. Spread it level and bake for 9–10 minutes, until puffy and set. Cool, then use the 3cm cutter to cut out 30 discs. Set aside.

To make the light pistachio Chantilly
Heat the milk and 135g of the double cream in a small saucepan over a low–medium heat until hot but not boiling. Remove the pan from the heat, add the gelatine mass and mix until melted.

Add the chocolate and the pistachio paste, mix to emulsify, then add the remaining 250g of cream. Mix to combine, cool the mixture, then cover it and chill until needed.

When you're ready to assemble, whip the Chantilly again until smooth, then spoon it into the piping bag with a 1.8cm nozzle.

To make the raspberry gel
Combine the raspberry purée, lemon purée or juice, sugar, Gelcrem Cold and water, and use a hand blender to mix until smooth. Cover, and chill until needed.

To make the pistachio chocolate
Melt the white chocolate in a heatproof bowl over a pan of barely simmering water. Stir until smooth, then remove from the heat.

Add the pistachio paste and mix until smooth and combined.

Brush the outside of the baked pistachio sablé with the pistachio chocolate and sprinkle with finely ground pistachio immediately, then leave to set.

To make the chocolate flowers
Melt the white chocolate in a heatproof bowl over a pan of barely simmering water. Stir until smooth, then remove from the heat.

Add the pinch of food colouring to make the white chocolate a very pale green colour and temper the chocolate following the instructions on page 200.

Lay an acetate sheet on your work surface and spread out the tempered chocolate to 1mm thick. Leave the chocolate to set at room temperature.

Using the 5cm flower cutter, stamp out flower shapes from the set chocolate, placing them on a baking sheet lined with baking paper as you go. Chill until needed.

To assemble
Place a pistachio sponge disc into each sablé shell and cover with about 5g of the raspberry gel. Pipe a bulb of pistachio Chantilly into the sablé to fill generously, and top with a chocolate flower disc.

Using a cocktail stick or bamboo skewer, carefully dip each frozen jelly into the warm neutral glaze to coat, allow any excess glaze to drip off. Place a coated jelly on top of each chocolate disc to finish.

PINK GUAVA AND PLUM CAKES

MAKES 40

For the plum gel
30g plum juice
120g water
4g caster sugar
1.2g agar agar
4g gelatine mass (see page 207)
54g candied plum, finely chopped

For the pink guava mixture
27g caster sugar
13g cornflour
140g pink guava purée
seeds from ½ vanilla bean
16g lemon purée or 3 teaspoons lemon juice
350g pink guava flesh, finely diced

For the shiso cream
335g 35%-fat cream or whipping cream
4 shiso leaves
50g 33% white chocolate (such as Valrhona Opalys), chopped
17g gelatine mass (see page 207)

For the sponge
105g caster sugar
35g canola oil
35g water
75g T55 or plain flour
2g baking powder
75g egg yolks
105g egg white

Drawing inspiration from Asian street food, this dessert infuses sour plum juice with the aniseed-mint profile of shiso – it is a reimagining of a classic flavour pairing. The result is a vibrant, tropical fruit-forward treat that's perfect for a summertime tea.

To make the plum gel
Combine the plum juice and water in a saucepan.

In a small bowl, mix together the sugar and agar agar. Add the mixture to the juice, stir to combine, then place the pan over a low–medium heat and bring to a boil.

Remove the pan from the heat. Add the gelatine mass and mix until melted and combined. Pour the mixture into a clean bowl or tub, cover and refrigerate until set.

Use a hand blender to blitz the set gel on high speed until smooth. Add the candied plum and stir to combine. Spoon 5g of the gel into each mini stone-shaped mould. Freeze for 1 hour until solid.

To make the pink guava mixture
Mix the sugar and cornflour in a small bowl and set aside.

In a small saucepan, heat the guava purée and vanilla seeds over a medium–low heat until the mixture reaches 40°C. Add the sugar and cornflour mixture and mix together until smooth.

With the pan over a low heat, and stirring continuously, bring the mixture to a boil. Cook until thickened and the cornflour has been cooked out. Pour the mixture into a clean bowl or tub and leave to cool.

Stir in the lemon purée or juice and the guava and spoon 5g into each mould on top of the set plum mixture. Freeze solid.

To make the shiso cream
In a small pan, heat half of the cream and all the shiso leaves to just below boiling. Remove from the heat, cover with cling film and leave to infuse for 15 minutes.

Strain the cream into a clean pan and reheat it to 60°C, then remove the pan from the heat. Add the white chocolate and, using a hand blender, blitz the mixture to a perfect emulsion. Add the gelatine mass and blitz again until melted and combined.

Continues overleaf

PINK GUAVA AND PLUM CAKES *CONTINUED*

For the almond sablé
90g unsalted butter, softened
70g icing sugar, sifted
a pinch of salt
40g eggs, lightly beaten
25g ground almonds
180g T45 or 00 flour

For the pink guava mousse
115g caster sugar
40g water
115g egg whites
75g strawberry purée
72g gelatine mass (see page 207)
380g guava purée
440g 35%-fat cream or whipping cream, softly whipped

For the light green chocolate dip
300g 33% white chocolate (such as Valrhona Opalys), broken up
225g cocoa butter
75g grapeseed or other neutral oil
a few drops of fat-soluble green food colouring

To finish
thinly sliced pink guava
plum powder, for dusting

You will also need
40 micro stone-shaped insert moulds: 5ml capacity
Piping bag fitted with a 5mm plain nozzle
23cm x 33cm baking tin, lined (base and sides) with baking paper
3cm round cutter
Piping bag fitted with a 1cm plain nozzle
40 Globe 26 moulds: 26ml capacity

Add the remaining cream and blitz to combine. Leave the mixture to cool, then spoon it into the piping bag fitted with a 5mm nozzle. Pipe 5g of the cream into each mini stone mould on top of the pink guava mixture and freeze again until solid.

To make the sponge
Heat the oven to 170°C fan.

Mix 35g of the caster sugar with the canola oil and water in a mixing bowl.

Sift the flour and baking powder into the bowl and whisk until smooth and thoroughly combined. Add the egg yolks and mix again until smooth.

In another mixing bowl or in a stand mixer fitted with the whisk, whisk the egg whites and remaining 70g of sugar until soft peaks form. Using a large metal spoon, gently fold the meringue into the cake batter.

Carefully spread the batter into the lined baking tin and cook for 8–10 minutes, until pale golden and set.

Leave the sponge to cool, then, using the 3cm round cutter, stamp out 40 discs. These will be your cake bases.

To make the almond sablé
Cream the butter, icing sugar and salt together in a stand mixer on low–medium speed until smooth and pale. Add the eggs, almonds and flour and mix again until incorporated and smooth.

Roll out the dough between two sheets of baking paper until 2mm thick. Place the dough on a baking sheet and chill for 30 minutes, until firm.

Heat the oven to 160°C fan. Line a baking sheet with baking paper.

Using the 3cm cutter, stamp out discs from the chilled sablé and arrange them on the lined baking sheet. Bake for 8–10 minutes, until crisp and golden brown at the edges.

To make the pink guava mousse
To make an Italian-meringue base for the mousse, tip the sugar into a small pan, add the water and bring it to a boil to dissolve the sugar. Continue to cook until the syrup reaches 118°C on a sugar thermometer.

Meanwhile, in a stand mixer fitted with the whisk, whisk the egg whites to soft peaks. Whisking slowly, very carefully pour the hot syrup into the bowl. Once all the syrup is in, whisk on medium speed until the meringue cools to 30°C.

In a small saucepan over a low heat, warm the strawberry purée to 60°C. Remove from the heat, add the gelatine mass and mix until melted and smooth. Add the guava purée and whisk until completely homogeneous.

Continues overleaf

PINK GUAVA AND PLUM CAKES *CONTINUED*

Using a large metal spoon, gently fold the purée mixture into the Italian meringue, followed by the softly whipped cream.

Spoon the mousse into the piping bag fitted with a 1 cm plain nozzle. Pipe 10g of the mousse mixture into a globe silicone mould. Unmould a frozen plum and guava insert and place the insert into the mousse. Cover with a sponge disc. Repeat for all the moulds. Freeze again for about 1 hour, or until solid.

Unmould the globes on to a lined baking tray and keep them frozen while you prepare the dipping mixture.

To make the light green chocolate dip
Combine the chocolate, cocoa butter and oil in a heatproof bowl and place it over a pan of barely simmering water. Stir until melted and smooth. A little at a time, add the green food colouring to make a very pale green colour and hold the mixture at a temperature of 27°C.

To assemble
Using a cocktail stick or bamboo skewer, dip each frozen cake into the green chocolate dip to coat, then transfer to a clean, baking-paper-lined tray to set at room temperature. Gently remove the cocktail sticks or skewers.

Place each cake on a sablé disc and decorate with thinly sliced pink guava and a dusting of plum powder.

HE LANGHAM
LONDON

CUSTARD CREAMS

MAKES 15

For the crème pâtissière
300g whole milk
seeds from ¼ vanilla bean
120g egg yolks
60g light brown soft sugar
17g cornflour
a pinch of salt

For the lemon sponge
finely grated zest of ½ unwaxed lemon
235g caster sugar
175g eggs, lightly beaten
100g 35%-fat cream or whipping cream
a pinch of salt
180g T45 or 00 flour
3.5g baking powder
70g unsalted butter, melted

For the feuilletine crunch
68g 35% white chocolate (such as Valrhona Dulcey), broken up
40g cocoa butter
90g feuilletine

For the coating
250g 35% white chocolate (such as Valrhona Dulcey), tempered (see page 200)
edible gold powder, for dusting

You will also need
Piping bag fitted with a 1cm plain nozzle
30cm x 40cm baking tin, lined (base and sides) with baking paper
15 rectangular/custard-cream moulds: 4cm x 5.5cm, 1.5–2cm deep

Nostalgia plays such an important part in the experience of Afternoon Tea, and what could be more nostalgically British than tea and biscuits? This cake is one that always delights our guests and so often evokes in them the fondest childhood memories.

To make the crème pâtissière
Warm the milk and vanilla seeds in a small saucepan over a medium–low heat to just below boiling. Meanwhile, in a bowl, whisk together the egg yolks, sugar, cornflour and salt until pale. Pour the hot milk into the bowl with the egg mixture, whisking until smooth and thoroughly combined. Return the mixture to the pan and cook over a low heat, stirring continuously, until thickened and the cornflour has been cooked out.

Remove the pan from the heat, strain the crème into a clean bowl, cover the surface with cling film, cool, then refrigerate. To assemble, spoon the crème into the piping bag with a 1cm plain nozzle.

To make the lemon sponge
In a stand mixer fitted with the paddle, mix the lemon zest with the sugar to extract the oil from the zests. Add the eggs, cream and salt and mix on medium speed to combine.

Sift the flour and baking powder into the bowl and fold them in using a large metal spoon. Add the melted butter and fold until combined and no dry patches remain.

Scoop the mixture into the lined baking tin. Cover and refrigerate overnight, if you wish, or bake immediately.

Heat the oven to 170°C fan. Bake the sponge for 20 minutes, until golden. Cool it in the tin, then cut it into neat 4cm x 5cm x 5mm rectangles.

To make the feuilletine crunch
Melt the chocolate with the cocoa butter in a heatproof bowl set over a pan of barely simmering water. Stir until smooth and remove from the heat. Mix in the feuilletine and spread out the mixture on a baking tray lined with baking paper. Leave to crystallise and set firm. Once the feuilletine has set, break it up into small pieces.

To assemble
Add a dessertspoonful of tempered white chocolate into each custard-cream shaped mould and tilt to coat evenly. Turn the mould over to allow any excess chocolate to drip out and leave to set at room temperature.

Sprinkle 8g of the feuilletine crunch into each mould. Pipe 12g of the crème pâtissière on top, then seal each custard cream with a lemon-sponge rectangle.

Chill the layered moulds for 10 minutes, then turn out the custard creams. Brush the shells with edible gold powder to serve.

STRAWBERRY PINK PEPPERCORN TARTS

MAKES 15

For the almond sablé
180g unsalted butter, softened
135g icing sugar, sifted
3g salt
75g eggs, lightly beaten
45g ground almonds
360g T45 or 00 flour

For the almond frangipane
125g unsalted butter, softened
125g icing sugar, sifted
125g ground almonds
60g eggs, lightly beaten
50g 35%-fat cream or whipping cream

For the strawberry and pink peppercorn confit
250g strawberries, hulled and sliced
60g caster sugar
250g strawberry purée
10g pectin NH
1 teaspoon lemon juice
4g pink peppercorns, lightly crushed

To finish
400g strawberries, hulled
icing sugar, for dusting

You will also need
Fifteen 5–6cm tart rings
5–6cm round cutter
2 piping bags fitted with a 1cm nozzle

To make the almond sablé
Cream the butter, icing sugar and salt together in a stand mixer on low–medium speed until smooth and pale. Add the eggs, almonds and flour and mix again until incorporated and smooth.

Roll out the dough between two sheets of baking paper until 3mm thick. Using the paper, slide the dough on to a baking sheet and refrigerate for 30 minutes, until firm.

Place the tart rings on a lined baking sheet. Using the cutter, stamp out 15 discs from the chilled dough and place one into each tart ring. Cut the remaining dough into 2cm-wide strips and use these to line the inside of each tart ring. Trim off the excess from the top to neaten.

Freeze the lined tart cases for 20 minutes. Meanwhile, heat the oven to 160°C fan.

Bake the tart rings from frozen (there's no need to use baking beans) for about 12 minutes, until golden. Leave the oven on.

To make the almond frangipane
In a mixing bowl, cream the butter and icing sugar until pale and light. Add the almonds and eggs, mix well to combine, then add the cream and mix again until smooth.

Scoop the mixture into a piping bag fitted with a 1cm nozzle and pipe it into the base of each tart case to half fill. Bake at 160°C fan for 5–6 minutes, until pale golden and set. Leave to cool.

To make the strawberry and pink peppercorn confit
In a small saucepan, cook the strawberries with 10g of the sugar over a low heat for about 5 minutes, until softened.

Add the purée, pectin and remaining 50g of sugar and bring to a boil.

Remove the pan from the heat, add the lemon juice and crushed pink peppercorns and leave to cool to room temperature.

Using a hand blender, blitz until smooth, then spoon the confit into the clean piping bag fitted with a 1cm nozzle. Pipe the confit into each tart on top of the frangipane to fill.

Continues overleaf

To assemble
Line a large baking tray with cling film or a silicone mat. Thinly slice the strawberries horizontally and arrange them in a neat, single rectangular layer on the tray.

Starting at one of the outside edges of the rectangle, use the cutter to stamp out neat discs from the strawberries. One disc at a time, leave the cutter in place and, using a wide palette knife or fish slice, lift the disc and carefully slide it on to the top of each tart. Slide away the knife or slice and remove the cutter. Repeat until all the tarts are covered with sliced strawberries.

A few minutes before serving, lightly dust the strawberry layer with icing sugar to create a shiny glaze.

ROSE AND LYCHEE BABAS

MAKES 15

For the soaking syrup
1 litre water
200g caster sugar
20 drops of rose essence or rose water

For the baba dough
65g whole milk
30g 35%-fat cream or whipping cream
15g fresh yeast
15g caster sugar
3g salt
200g T45 or 00 flour
100g eggs, lightly beaten
60g unsalted butter, melted

For the mascarpone cream
50g mascarpone
30g caster sugar
2 drops of rose essence or rose water, or to taste
250g 35%-fat cream or whipping cream

For the lychee jelly
50g caster sugar
12g pectin NH
500g lychee purée
12g citric acid or 2 teaspoons lemon juice
red food-colouring powder

To finish
edible red rose petals

You will also need
Piping bag fitted with a 1cm plain nozzle
15 oval silicone moulds: 5.5cm long and 1.5cm deep
Piping bag fitted with a 5mm plain nozzle

To make the soaking syrup
Pour the water into a saucepan and add the sugar. Place the pan over a medium heat and bring the water to a boil, stirring to dissolve the sugar.

Remove the pan from the heat, add the rose essence or rose water, pour the syrup into a large mixing bowl and leave to cool to room temperature.

To make the baba dough
Warm the milk and cream in a small saucepan to 25°C and pour the mixture into the bowl of a stand mixer fitted with a dough hook.

Crumble in the yeast, add the sugar and salt and mix to thoroughly combine and dissolve the yeast. Sift in the flour and mix to combine.

Add the eggs and mix slowly without adding too much body to the mixture.

Remove the bowl from the stand mixer and pour the melted butter on top of the baba mixture. Do not mix but leave the dough to rest for 20 minutes, then, using a wooden spoon, mix until smooth.

Cover the bowl and leave the dough to prove at room temperature for about 1 hour, or until doubled in volume.

Scoop the mixture into the piping bag fitted with a 1cm plain nozzle. Pipe the dough into the moulds, half-filling each. Cover the moulds loosely with a sheet of baking paper or a silicone air mat (this will help them rise evenly) and leave them to prove at room temperature for about 1 hour, until doubled in volume.

Heat the oven to 170°C fan.

Remove the baking paper or mat and bake the babas for about 12 minutes, until risen and golden brown. Remove the babas from the moulds and leave them to cool on a wire rack. Wash and dry the moulds.

Once they are cold, add the babas to the bowl with the soaking syrup and leave to soak overnight.

To make the mascarpone cream
Mix together mascarpone and sugar. A little a time, add the rose essence or rose water, tasting as you go and stopping when you're happy with the flavour.

Add the cream and whisk until it will hold a firm peak. Cover the bowl and chill the cream until needed.

To make the lychee jelly
In a small bowl, whisk together the sugar and pectin NH.

Continues overleaf

ROSE AND LYCHEE BABAS *CONTINUED*

In a small saucepan, bring the lychee purée to a boil over a low–medium heat. Add the sugar and pectin mixture and stir to combine. Return the mixture to a boil, whisking continuously, then remove the pan from the heat and add the citric acid or lemon juice. A little at a time, add the red food colouring, blitzing with a hand blender until you reach the desired colour and the mixture is smooth.

To assemble
Remove the babas from the syrup and leave them to drain on a wire rack for a few minutes.

Half fill each clean mould with the lychee jelly.

Place each drained baba into a jelly and refrigerate for at least 2 hours to set.

Pop out the baba-jellies from the moulds and place them on a tray, ensuring that the jelly is uppermost.

Spoon the whipped cream into the piping bag fitted with a 5mm nozzle and pipe a neat line on top of each baba. Decorate with a rose petal to serve.

DECIDEDLY MADELEINE

MAKES 36

For the financier
265g unsalted butter
255g T45 or 00 flour, plus extra for dusting
200g caster sugar
25g light brown soft sugar
a pinch of salt
288g eggs, lightly beaten
40g clear honey or inverted sugar
seeds from ¼ vanilla bean
7g baking powder

For the passionfruit pâté de fruits
255g passionfruit purée
7g pectin NH
350g caster sugar
38g liquid glucose
10g citric acid or 18g lemon juice
a little melted butter, for greasing

To finish
250g 64% dark chocolate (such as Valrhona Manjari), broken up
bronze or gold edible powder, for dusting

You will also need
3 x 12-hole madeleine moulds (we use metal moulds to bake the madeleines and the same size silicone moulds to set the pâté de fruits, but at home you could use just a silicone mould)

These madeleines come with a real zing of flavour from the passionfruit. The chocolate shell adds a crunch to highlight the soft, fabulous financier sponge.

To make the financier
In a small saucepan, melt the butter over a low–medium heat. Brush the madeleine moulds with a little of the melted butter to thoroughly coat. Dust with flour, turn the moulds upside down and tap them sharply on the work surface to remove any excess. Place the moulds in the fridge while you prepare the financier mixture.

In a large mixing bowl, combine the caster sugar, light brown sugar and the salt. Add the eggs, honey or inverted sugar and vanilla seeds and whisk to combine. Sift the flour and baking powder into the bowl and mix until no dry patches remain. Add the remaining melted butter and beat again until smooth and thoroughly combined. Cover the bowl and refrigerate the mixture overnight.

When you're ready to bake, heat the oven to 180°C fan. Spoon the chilled financier mixture into the prepared moulds until each one is just under half filled.

Bake the madeleines for 12 minutes, until well risen and golden brown. Leave to cool in the moulds for 2 minutes, then turn them out on to a wire rack to cool completely.

To make the passionfruit pâté de fruits
In a small saucepan, warm the passionfruit purée over a medium–low heat to 40°C.

In a bowl, combine the pectin with 30g of the caster sugar. Add this to the purée and bring to a boil. Add the glucose and the remaining 320g of sugar to the pan and cook over a medium heat, until the mixture reaches 106°C. Add the citric acid or lemon juice and mix to combine. Grease the madeleine moulds with butter.

Pour 8–10g of the mixture into each of the greased moulds. Immediately push a baked sponge into the jelly, shell side down and leave to set at room temperature (about 1–2 hours). Remove from the moulds.

To assemble
Temper the dark chocolate following the instructions on page 200.

One at a time, dip the jelly side of each sponge into the tempered chocolate until neatly coated (try not to get any chocolate on the sponge side).

Tap to remove the excess chocolate and place the madeleine, chocolate side uppermost, on a sheet of baking paper. Repeat for all the madeleines. Leave them at room temperature for the chocolate to set, then brush with a gold or bronze edible powder to serve.

BREAD AND BUTTER

MAKES 12

For the caramel brioche
190g T45 or 00 flour, sifted
50g T55 or plain flour, sifted
50g whole milk
8g fresh yeast
4g salt
50g caramel powder or dark muscovado sugar
70g eggs, lightly beaten
50g unsalted butter, softened

For the blood orange glaze
200g blood orange purée
80g caster sugar
50g liquid glucose
12g pectin NH
2 teaspoons lemon juice

For the almond sablé
90g unsalted butter, softened
70g icing sugar, sifted
a pinch of salt
40g eggs, lightly beaten
25g ground almonds
185g T45 or 00 flour

For the diplomat cream
200g whole milk
seeds from ¼ vanilla bean
50g egg yolks
45g light brown soft sugar
7g cornflour
15g cocoa butter
15g gelatine mass (see page 207)
50g 35%-fat cream or whipping cream

This jewel of a cake is all about serving familiar flavours in unexpected ways. It is a refined take on a classic, British bread-and-butter pudding.

To make the caramel brioche
Tip all the ingredients apart from the butter into a stand mixer fitted with the dough hook. Mix on low speed for 8 minutes, until smooth and thoroughly combined.

Little by little, add the butter. Once it is all added, mix for a further 2 minutes, until the dough is smooth and shiny. Cover the bowl and leave the dough to rise at room temperature for about 1½ hours, until doubled in volume.

Turn out the dough on to a lightly floured work surface. Shape the dough into a ball and place it in the lined loaf tin. Cover loosely and leave to prove at room temperature for about 1 hour, or until doubled in volume.

Meanwhile, heat the oven to 170°C fan.

Bake the proved brioche for about 35 minutes, until well risen and golden brown. Remove the brioche from the tin and leave it to cool in a wire rack.

To make the blood orange glaze
In a small saucepan over a low–medium heat, warm the purée, then add the sugar, glucose and pectin, stir to combine, and bring the mixture to a boil. Remove the pan from the heat, add the lemon juice and mix to combine.

Leave the glaze to cool, then cover and chill until needed.

To make the almond sablé
Mix the butter, icing sugar and salt together in a stand mixer fitted with the paddle, on low speed until pale and light. Add the eggs, almonds and flour and mix again until smooth and thoroughly combined.

Roll out the sablé between two sheets of baking paper until 2mm thick. Using the paper, slide the sablé on to a baking sheet, leaving the paper sheets in place. Freeze for about 30 minutes, until firm. Remove the top sheet of paper and cut the chilled sablé into twelve 4cm squares. Arrange these on a lined baking sheet and refrigerate for 20 minutes while you heat the oven to 160°C fan.

Bake the sablés for about 12 minutes, until golden, then leave to cool.

Continues overleaf

For the crème Anglaise
170g whole milk
170g 35%-fat cream or whipping cream
65g egg yolks
35g caster sugar

You will also need
900g loaf tin, greased and lined (base and ends) with baking paper
Piping bag fitted with a 1cm plain nozzle
Twelve 3cm cube moulds

To make the diplomat cream
In a small saucepan, heat the milk with the vanilla seeds over a medium–low heat until just below boiling.

Meanwhile, in a bowl whisk together the egg yolks, sugar and cornflour until pale.

Add a quarter of the hot milk to the egg mixture and whisk until smooth. Then, return the mixture to the pan and cook over a low–medium heat, stirring continuously, until the sauce thickens and the cornflour has been cooked out.

Remove the pan from the heat and add the cocoa butter and gelatine mass and blend until smooth. Strain the pastry cream into a clean bowl and leave to cool. Cover and chill until needed.

Whip the cream until it holds soft peaks, then fold this into the cooled pastry cream. Spoon the diplomat cream into the piping bag fitted with a 1cm plain nozzle and chill until needed.

To make the crème Anglaise
Heat the milk and cream in a small saucepan over a medium–low heat to just below boiling.

Meanwhile, in a bowl, whisk together the egg yolks and sugar until pale. Pour the hot milk into the bowl, whisking continuously until smooth. Return the mixture to the pan and cook over a low heat, stirring continuously until thickened.

Remove the pan from the heat and strain the crème Anglaise into a clean bowl. Cover the surface with cling film and leave to cool to room temperature.

To assemble
Heat the oven to 160°C fan. Line a baking sheet with baking paper.

Cut half of the cold brioche into twelve 2cm cubes and soak these in the crème Anglaise for 30 seconds.

Slice the remaining brioche into wafer-thin slices. Arrange these on a lined baking sheet and toast them in the oven for about 4 minutes, until crisp.

Pipe about 20g of the diplomat cream into each of the cube moulds. Push a soaked and drained brioche into the cream in each one, cover with more diplomat cream and smooth over. Freeze the filled moulds for about 2 hours, until firm.

Carefully remove the frozen diplomat cubes from the moulds, placing them on a wire rack set over a sheet of baking paper (to catch the drips).

In a saucepan, heat the blood orange glaze to 35°C and pour this over the cubes to coat. Leave to set at room temperature, and leave the cubes to fully defrost.

To serve, place each cube on a square of almond sablé and decorate with a toasted and curved slice of brioche.

PRALINE PARIS-BREST

MAKES ABOUT 75

For the whipped pecan cream
210g whole milk
37g 0%-fat milk powder
10g caster sugar
33g gelatine mass (see page 207)
255g pecan praline
135g cocoa butter, melted
210g 35%-fat cream or whipping cream
125g egg whites
a pinch of salt

For the choux pastry
150g whole milk
150g water
130g unsalted butter, cubed
18g caster sugar
6g salt
180g T55 or plain flour, sifted
290g eggs, lightly beaten

For the craquelin
95g light brown soft sugar
75g unsalted butter, softened
95g T55 or plain flour

To finish
edible gold leaf
100g hazelnuts, blanched and toasted

You will also need
2 piping bags, each fitted with a plain 5mm nozzle
2cm round cutter
1cm round cutter

To make the whipped pecan cream
In a small saucepan, heat the milk with the milk powder and sugar over a low–medium heat and bring to a boil.

Remove the pan from the heat, add the gelatine mass and mix until melted. Add the pecan praline, cocoa butter, cream, egg whites and salt and use a hand blender to blitz until smooth.

Transfer the mixture to a bowl and leave it overnight in the fridge to thicken and crystallise. When you're ready to assemble, spoon the pecan cream into a piping bag fitted with a 5mm nozzle.

To make the choux pastry and craquelin
Pour the milk into a small saucepan, add the water, butter, caster sugar and salt and place over a medium heat to melt the butter. Bring the mixture to a boil, then immediately remove the pan from the heat.

Tip in the sifted flour and beat well until smooth and thoroughly incorporated.

Place the pan back over a low heat and stir with a spatula for about 1 minute, until the mixture dries out, is smooth and cleanly leaves the side of the pan.

Scoop the mixture into the bowl of a stand mixer fitted with the paddle and leave to cool for about 5 minutes, or until 40°C.

Mixing continuously on low–medium speed, little by little, add the beaten eggs until they have all been added and the mixture is glossy, smooth, reluctantly drops off a spoon and holds a firm peak.

Cover and leave the choux pastry to rest at room temperature for 2 hours.

Meanwhile, prepare the craquelin. In a small bowl beat the brown sugar with the butter and flour until smooth. Roll out the mixture between two sheets of baking paper until 2mm thick. Using the baking paper, slide the craquelin dough on to a baking sheet and freeze with the baking paper in place for 30 minutes, until firm.

Meanwhile, heat the oven to 170°C fan. Line two large baking sheets with baking paper (or use silicone air mats).

Continues overleaf

PRALINE PARIS-BREST *CONTINUED*

Scoop the rested choux pastry into the remaining piping bag fitted with a 5mm plain nozzle and pipe approximately 5g mounds on to the prepared baking sheets (or the air mats). You should get about 75 mounds altogether.

Using the 2cm round cutter, stamp out about 75 discs from the frozen craquelin and place one on top of each choux mound.

Bake the choux buns for about 17 minutes, until golden brown, well risen and crisp. Leave to cool before filling.

To assemble
Cut the choux buns in half and, using the 1cm round cutter, stamp out and discard a disc from the middle of each top half.

Pipe bulbs of pecan cream into the bottom half of each choux bun. Place the choux bun ring on top. Pipe another bulb of cream into the space in the middle and decorate each one with a toasted hazelnut and piece of edible gold leaf. Finish with a grating of toasted hazelnut.

CHAPTER THREE

SHARING CAKES

THE LANGHAM PINK BATTENBERG

MAKES 15

For the vanilla pound cake
200g unsalted butter, softened
150g caster sugar
5g vanilla paste
200g eggs, lightly beaten
215g T55 or plain flour
5g baking powder

For the rose pound cake
200g unsalted butter
150g caster sugar
1g fat-soluble pink food-colouring powder
200g eggs, lightly beaten
5g rose extract
215g T55 or plain flour
5g baking powder

For the vanilla ganache
700g 33% white chocolate (such as Valrhona Opalys), chopped
100g cocoa butter
300g whole milk
200g 35%-fat cream or whipping cream
½ vanilla bean, split
16g caster sugar
6g X58 pectin
50g unsalted butter, softened

For the raspberry confit
400g raspberry purée
100g caster sugar
6g pectin NH

Battenberg cake was created in 1884 to celebrate the marriage of Queen Victoria's granddaughter (also named Victoria) to Prince Louis of Battenberg. As a result, it symbolises festivity and royal elegance. The Langham version features a delicate rose flavour, which is inspired by our iconic Rose Garden in London.

Make the vanilla pound cake
Heat the oven to 170°C fan.

Cream the butter, sugar and vanilla paste together in a stand mixer fitted with the paddle, on medium speed for 3–4 minutes, until light and pale.

Gradually add the beaten eggs, mixing well between each addition. Sift the flour and baking powder into the bowl and, using a large metal spoon, fold in the flour until thoroughly incorporated and the mixture is smooth.

Spoon the cake batter into the tin, spread it level and bake for 20–25 minutes, until golden, well risen and a wooden skewer inserted into the centre comes out clean.

Leave the cake to cool in the tin, then turn it out on to a clean sheet of baking paper.

To make the rose pound cake
Wash, then line the cake tin again.
To make the rose cake, repeat the method for the vanilla pound cake, adding the pink colouring with the butter and sugar, and adding the rose extract after the eggs.

To make the vanilla ganache
Melt the chocolate and cocoa butter in a heatproof bowl over a pan of barely simmering water. Stir to combine, remove from the heat and set aside.

In a small saucepan, heat the milk, cream and vanilla bean over a low heat, until the mixture reaches 45°C.

Meanwhile, in a bowl, mix together the sugar and pectin and when the milk mixture reaches the required temperature, add the sugar mixture to the pan. Mix to combine, increase the heat a little and bring the mixture to a boil.

Immediately add the cream mixture to the melted chocolate and leave it to cool to 40–45°C. Add the butter, then use a hand blender to blitz to a perfect emulsion. Cover the ganache and refrigerate it for 2 hours before using.

Continues overleaf

THE LANGHAM PINK BATTENBERG *CONTINUED*

For the rose syrup
150g caster sugar
150g water
2–3 drops of rose essence

For the pink chocolate coating
350g 31% white chocolate (such as Valrhona Satilia Blanche), chopped
150g canola oil
a pinch of fat-soluble pink food-colouring powder

For the pink velvet spray
250g 31% white chocolate (such as Valrhona Satilia Blanche), chopped
250g cocoa butter
a pinch of fat-soluble pink food-colouring powder

You will also need
20cm x 30cm baking tin, greased and lined (base and sides) with baking paper
Spray gun

To make the raspberry confit
Place the raspberry purée into a small saucepan.

In a small bowl, mix the sugar and pectin together, then sprinkle the mixture on to the raspberry purée. Mix to combine, then place the pan over a low–medium heat. Bring the mixture to a boil and immediately remove the pan from the heat. Pour the mixture into a bowl and leave it at room temperature to cool and set. Once the mixture has gelled, use a hand blender to blitz it. This will soften its texture.

To make the rose syrup
Tip the sugar into a small saucepan and add the water. Place the pan over a low–medium heat and bring the liquid to a boil to dissolve the sugar. Remove from the heat, add the rose extract and leave to cool.

To make the pink chocolate coating
Melt the chocolate and canola oil in a heatproof bowl set over a pan of barely simmering water until combined. Add the food colouring and mix to combine. Remove from the heat and set aside.

To make the pink velvet spray
Melt together the chocolate, cocoa butter and food colouring in a heatproof bowl set over a pan of barely simmering water. Stir until smooth. Spoon into the spray gun.

To assemble
Trim the sides of both of the cakes to neaten and, using a palette knife, thinly spread raspberry confit evenly over the top of the vanilla cake.

Place the rose cake on top, then slice the cake sandwich into 10 rectangular strips, each measuring 3cm x 18cm. Working from the left-hand side, spread raspberry confit over the cut side of the first strip and flip the next slice over so that the raspberry cake is now on the bottom. Press the two strips together to create a neat grid with a cross of confit in the centre. Repeat to create 5 neat Battenberg cake strips.

Brush rose syrup evenly all over the assembled cakes and place them on a lined baking sheet. Freeze for 30 minutes to set.

Using a palette knife, spread a 2mm-thick layer of the chilled ganache around three sides of each cake and freeze again for 30 minutes, until firm.

Turn the cakes over, spread a 2mm layer of ganache over the remaining side and return to the freezer for 30 minutes.

Place the cakes on a wire rack and warm the pink chocolate coating to 28°C. Pour the coating over the cakes to glaze evenly. Leave the cakes to sit for 10 minutes, or until the coating sets.

Spray the pink velvet spray over each cake to coat, then slice each cake strip into 6cm lengths (giving 15 small cakes altogether), to serve.

LANGHAM

PINK GUAVA ST. HONORÉ

MAKES 30

For the inverted puff pastry
You will need only two thirds of this pastry quantity but it's hard to make in smaller amounts. Freeze any unused pastry for another time.

For the detrempe (base dough)
420g T55 or plain flour, plus extra for dusting
18g salt
135g unsalted butter
180g water
3g white vinegar

For the beurrage
180g T45 or 00 flour
450g unsalted butter
icing sugar, for dusting

For the guava confit
290g pink guava purée
50g strawberry purée
45g caster sugar
5g pectin NH
10g lemon purée or 2 teaspoons lemon juice

For the oolong tea Chantilly
700g 35%-fat cream or whipping cream
35g Jing–Oolong tea leaves
30g gelatine mass (see page 207)
230g 33% white chocolate (such as Valrhona Opalys), chopped

For the pink guava Chantilly
300g guava confit
300g vanilla Chantilly (see page 208; ½ quantity will be more than enough)

A reinvention of one of The Langham's most beloved afternoon-tea treats, this St. Honoré pairs the pink guavas of Guangdong province, China, with light, floral oolong tea from Fujian.

To make the inverted puff pastry
To make the detrempe, place the flour, salt and butter in a stand mixer fitted with the dough hook and slowly mix everything to loosely combine. Add the water and vinegar and keep mixing for 3 minutes on low speed, then increase the speed to medium and mix for about 10 minutes, until the dough is smooth, elastic and will create a clear windowpane when a little of it is stretched between your fingers.

Once the dough is ready, flatten it in a neat rectangle, cover and refrigerate overnight.

Immediately prepare the beurrage. Combine the flour and butter in the stand mixer fitted with the paddle and mix until smooth. Transfer the mixture to a large sheet of baking paper, cover with a second sheet of paper and roll the beurrage into a neat rectangle that is of even thickness and is twice as large as the detrempe. Cover the beurrage and refrigerate overnight.

Place the beurrage on a floured work surface and place the dough on top in the middle of it. Fold the beurrage around the dough to enclose it completely. Cover and chill again for 20 minutes.

If you're rolling the pastry by hand, flour the work surface and roll the dough to a long, neat rectangle that is three times as long as it is wide. Fold the top of the rectangle down to cover the middle third and the bottom third up to cover this, as if you were folding a letter. This is a single fold. Cover and refrigerate for 30 minutes.

Repeat this folding and chilling a further 4 times to make a total of 5 single folds. Then, chill the dough for 2 hours or until needed.

If you are using a dough breaker, roll out the dough to a long rectangle. In total make 5 single folds, resting the dough in the fridge for at least 1 hour between each single fold.

Once the folds are complete and the dough has rested, separate out two thirds for use and freeze the remainder for another time. Flour the work surface again and roll out the dough to 3mm thick. Transfer the dough to a lined baking sheet and refrigerate it for 1 hour.

Heat the oven to 190°C fan. Line 2 large baking sheets with baking paper.

Continues overleaf

PINK GUAVA ST. HONORÉ *CONTINUED*

For the choux pastry
150g whole milk
150g water
130g unsalted butter, cubed
18g caster sugar
6g salt
180g T55 or plain flour, sifted
290g eggs, lightly beaten

For the pink craquelin
110g caster sugar
90g unsalted butter, softened
4 drops of pink colouring
110g T55 or plain flour

You will also need
8cm round cutter
2 piping bags, each fitted with a 5mm plain nozzle
2cm round cutter
Piping bag fitted with a 1cm closed star nozzle

Cut the dough into 30cm x 40cm rectangles, place these on the lined baking sheets. Dust the pastry with icing sugar. Cover the rectangles with another sheet of baking paper and place another baking sheet on top of each batch. (Alternatively, place the dough in between two sheets of silicone air mats.)

Bake the pastry for 30–35 minutes or until crisp and golden.

Using the 8cm round cutter, stamp out 30 discs from the baked puff pastry. Set aside.

To make the guava confit
Tip the guava and strawberry purées into a small saucepan and stir to combine.

In a small bowl, mix the sugar and pectin together, then sprinkle the mixture on to the fruit purées.

Using a hand blender, blitz until homogeneous, then warm the mixture over a low–medium heat to 85°C. Add the lemon purée or juice and, stirring continuously, bring to a boil.

Pour the mixture into a clean bowl and leave it at room temperature to cool and set. Once set, blend until smooth. Scoop into a piping bag fitted with a 5mm nozzle.

To make the oolong tea Chantilly
Combine the cream and tea leaves in a jug and chill for 12 hours.

Pour the chilled tea and cream into a small saucepan and bring the mixture to a boil over a low heat. Simmer very gently for 5 minutes to infuse.

Strain the tea mixture into a clean bowl to remove the leaves, then pour half of the infused cream into a clean pan and heat to 60°C. Remove the pan from the heat, add the gelatine mass and mix until smooth and to melt the gelatine.

Add the white chocolate and, using a hand blender, blitz to a perfect emulsion. Add the remaining infused cream and mix to combine.

Pour the Chantilly into a clean bowl, cool, then cover and chill for 12 hours or overnight.

Make the pink guava Chantilly
Add the guava confit to the vanilla Chantilly and mix to combine. Cover and chill until needed.

To make the choux pastry and the craquelin
To make the choux pastry, pour the milk into a small saucepan, add the water, butter, sugar and salt and place the pan over a medium heat. Melt the butter, then bring to a boil. Immediately remove the pan from the heat.

Add the sifted flour and beat well until smooth and thoroughly incorporated.

Place the pan back over a low heat and stir with a spatula for about 1 minute, until the mixture dries out, is smooth and cleanly leaves the side of the pan.

Scoop the mixture into the stand mixer fitted with the paddle and leave it to cool for 5 minutes to 40°C.

A little at a time, add the beaten eggs, mixing continuously on low–medium speed until the mixture is glossy, smooth, reluctantly drops off a spoon and will hold a firm peak.

Cover the bowl and leave the choux pastry to rest at room temperature for 2 hours.

Meanwhile, prepare the craquelin. In a small bowl beat the sugar, soft butter, pink food colouring and flour together until smooth. Roll out the mixture between two sheets of baking paper to 2mm thick. Slide the craquelin on to a baking sheet and freeze for 30 minutes, until firm.

Heat the oven to 170°C fan. Line 3 large baking sheets with baking paper.

Scoop the choux batter into the remaining piping bag fitted with a 5mm nozzle and pipe 150 approximately 5g mounds on to the lined baking sheets.

Using the 2cm round cutter, stamp out 150 discs from the frozen pink craquelin and place one on top of each choux mound.

Bake the craquelin-topped choux buns for about 17 minutes, until the buns are golden brown, well risen and crisp. Leave to cool before filling.

To assemble

Using a skewer, make a small hole on the underside of each choux bun and pipe guava pink Chantilly into each bun to fill.

Spoon the oolong Chantilly into the piping bag fitted with a 1cm closed star nozzle.

Place 4 choux buns on top of each puff-pastry disc and pipe a neat bulb of oolong Chantilly in between each bun and one bulb in the centre.

Pipe the remaining guava confit in the middle and cover with another 4 bulbs of oolong Chantilly, each on top of a choux bun, and another in the centre. Top with a fifth choux bun to finish.

HONEY CAKE

MAKES 6

4g finely grated lemon zest (about 2 unwaxed lemons)
4g finely grated orange zest (about 2 oranges)
325g dark muscovado sugar
a pinch of salt
240g eggs, lightly beaten
150g 35%-fat cream or whipping cream
260g T45 or 00 flour
5g baking powder
100g unsalted butter, melted

To assemble
220–250g clear honey
100g pearl sugar

You will also need
Six 10cm round silicone moulds, 3cm deep, greased with butter and lined with baking paper

An unapologetic celebration of honey, this cake is quite simply sweet, sticky and utterly, perfectly delicious.

In a stand mixer fitted with the paddle, combine the lemon and orange zests with the sugar and salt and mix on low speed for 1 minute to extract the oil from the zests.

Gradually add the eggs and cream to the bowl, mixing continuously until smooth. Sift the flour and baking powder into the bowl and mix until almost combined. Add the melted butter and mix again until smooth. Bake immediately, or cover and chill the mixture overnight.

Heat the oven to 160°C fan.

Weigh 180g of the cake mixture into each mould and bake the cakes for 30–35 minutes, until well risen and a skewer inserted into the middle of each comes out clean.

Leave the cakes to rest for 3–4 minutes in the moulds, then remove them and leave to cool on a wire rack for 10 minutes.

To assemble
Drizzle the warm cakes with the honey, leave to cool to room temperature, then scatter with pearl sugar to serve.

COCONUT TEA CAKE

MAKES 8

For the sponge
140g T45 or 00 flour, sifted
175g caster sugar
55g desiccated coconut
3g baking powder
a pinch of salt
125g eggs, lightly beaten
75g 35%-fat cream or whipping cream
50g unsalted butter, melted

For the coconut dacquoise
100g egg whites
a pinch of salt
50g caster sugar
75g desiccated coconut
40g icing sugar, sifted
10g cornflour

For the Malibu ganache
140g coconut purée (or 70g coconut milk and 70g coconut cream)
20g liquid glucose
380g 35% white chocolate (such as Valrhona Ivoire), chopped
15g Malibu
25g unsalted butter

For the coconut glaze
500g 35% white chocolate (such as Valrhona Ivoire), chopped
50g canola or neutral oil
100g desiccated coconut

You will also need
Eight 10cm round silicone moulds, 3cm deep
Piping bag fitted with a 5mm plain nozzle

To make the sponge
Heat the oven to 160°C fan.

In a large mixing bowl, mix together the flour, sugar, coconut, baking powder and salt. Add the eggs, cream and melted butter and beat until smooth and combined.

Pour 75g of the sponge mixture into each mould and bake for 13–14 minutes, until risen, golden brown and light. Leave the cakes to cool for 2–3 minutes, then unmould them and cool them on a wire rack. Wash and dry the moulds.

To make the coconut dacquoise
Heat the oven to 160°C fan.

In a stand mixer fitted with the whisk, whisk the egg whites with the salt on medium speed, to soft peaks. A little at a time, add the caster sugar, whisking continuously until the meringue holds soft peaks again.

Using a large metal spoon, fold in the coconut, icing sugar and cornflour. Scoop the mixture into the piping bag fitted with a 5mm nozzle and pipe 30g into each clean mould. Bake for about 20 minutes, until crisp. Remove the dacquoise from the moulds and leave to cool. Wash and dry the moulds.

To make the Malibu ganache
In a small saucepan over a low–medium heat, bring the coconut purée (or coconut milk and cream) and glucose to a boil.

Meanwhile, partially melt the white chocolate (some molten, some firm) in a heatproof bowl set over a pan of barely simmering water. Remove the bowl from the heat and pour in the coconut mixture. Use a rubber spatula to mix and emulsify. Stir in the Malibu and leave the ganache to cool to 50°C. Add the butter and, using a hand blender, blitz until perfectly smooth. You can use the ganache immediately.

To begin the assembly
Spoon the ganache equally into the clean moulds. Place a dacquoise on top of each, then add a cake. Cover with cling film and freeze until firm (about 2 hours).

To make the coconut glaze
Melt the chocolate in a heatproof bowl set over a pan of barely simmering water until it reaches to 45°C. Remove from the heat, add the oil, then mix to combine. Cool the glaze to 30°C.

To finish the assembly
Turn the cakes out of the moulds. One by one, dip the ganache layer into the glaze to coat and place each cake on a wire rack. Scatter with desiccated coconut and leave to set before serving.

VANILLA CHEESECAKE

MAKES 6

For the sablé base
105g unsalted butter, softened
135g ground hazelnuts
105g caster sugar
105g T45 or 00 flour, sifted
a pinch of salt

For the vanilla cheesecake filling
460g cream cheese
120g caster sugar
seeds from ¼ vanilla bean
100g eggs, lightly beaten
60g soured cream
55g 35%-fat cream or whipping cream
6g cornflour

For the chocolate collar
200g 33% white chocolate (such as Valrhona Opalys), chopped

To finish
seasonal fresh fruit
micro herbs, such as basil

You will also need
Six 9cm ring moulds, 5cm deep
6 acetate sheets, measuring 30cm x 6cm

To make the sablé base
Heat the oven to 160°C fan.

In a mixing bowl, cream the butter until soft and light. Add the remaining ingredients and mix well until thoroughly combined.

Scatter the mixture evenly on to a lined baking tray and bake for 15–18 minutes, turning the mixture halfway through, until evenly golden brown. Leave to cool to room temperature, then blitz in a food processor to a fine crumb.

Wrap each of the ring moulds with a double thickness of foil to cover the base and outsides, and grease the inside of the rings. Place the rings into a shallow roasting tin. Using the back of a teaspoon, press 75g of the sablé crumb into each of the lined rings to cover the bases in an even layer. Chill for 1 hour, until firm.

To make the vanilla cheesecake filling
In a mixing bowl using a rubber spatula, beat the cream cheese, sugar and vanilla seeds until combined.

Little by little, add each of the eggs, soured cream and cream. Mix until smooth and without incorporating air bubbles into the mixture. Add the cornflour and mix until smooth again.

To bake and begin the assembly
Heat the oven to 150°C fan.

Carefully spoon 130g of the cheesecake mixture into each ring on top of the base. Spread it level and pour hot water into the roasting tin to come halfway up the outsides of the rings. Bake the cheesecakes for about 35 minutes, until set.

Cool the cheesecakes to room temperature, then remove them from the roasting tin (still in the moulds), cover and chill overnight.

To make the chocolate collar
On the day of serving, melt the chocolate in a heatproof bowl set over a pan of barely simmering water. Stir until smooth, remove from the heat and leave to cool slightly.

Lay the measured acetate sheets on flat baking sheets. Using an offset palette knife, spread the melted chocolate into a 1–2mm thick layer across all the sheets to coat them entirely. Leave until almost set.

To finish the assembly
To serve, unmould the cheesecakes and wrap the outside of each in a chocolate collar with the acetate on the outside. Chill to set firm, then carefully peel away the acetate. Serve topped with seasonal fresh fruit and a few micro herb leaves.

CARAÏBE TEA CAKE

MAKES 8

For the caraïbe tea cakes
85g unsalted butter
75g 66% dark chocolate
125g caster sugar
75g ground almonds
120g T45 or 00 flour, sifted
25g cocoa powder, plus extra for dusting
6g baking powder
250g eggs, lightly beaten
75g inverted sugar or clear honey
120g 35%-fat cream or whipping cream
8 chocolate curls, to decorate (optional)

For the caraïbe crémeux
200g whole milk
200g 35%-fat cream or whipping cream
80g egg yolks
40g caster sugar
200g 66% dark chocolate (such as Valrhona Caraïbe), chopped

For the rocher glaze
225g milk chocolate
50g canola or other neutral oil

You will also need
Eight 10cm round silicone moulds, 3cm deep
Piping bag fitted with a 1cm plain nozzle

To make the caraïbe tea cakes
Heat the oven to 180°C fan.

Melt the butter and chocolate together in a heatproof bowl over a pan of barely simmering water. Stir until smooth and remove from the heat.

In a stand mixer fitted with the paddle, combine the caster sugar, almonds, flour, cocoa and baking powder.

Add the eggs, inverted sugar or honey, the cream and the chocolate mixture and mix on medium speed for 1–2 minutes, until smooth and thoroughly combined.

Pour 120g of the cake mixture into each of the moulds and bake the cakes for 17–18 minutes, until risen and light. Leave the cakes to cool for 2–3 minutes, then unmould them and cool them on a wire rack. Wash and dry the moulds.

To make the caraïbe crémeux
Pour the milk and cream into a small saucepan over a low–medium heat and bring to just below boiling point.

In a small bowl ,whisk the yolks and sugar together until combined and slightly paler in colour. Whisking continuously, pour the hot milk and cream mixture into the egg mixture. Mix until smooth, then return everything to the pan and cook, stirring, until the sauce reaches 80–84°C.

Strain the sauce into a clean bowl and leave to cool slightly.

Add the chocolate to the bowl with the sauce, leave for 5 minutes to melt, then use a hand blender to blitz to a perfect emulsion. Leave the crémeux to cool completely, then cover and chill until firm.

To begin the assembly
Scoop the crémeux into the piping bag fitted with a 1cm nozzle.

Pipe 90g of the crémeux into each clean mould. Trim the top of the cakes to level, then add one cake top down into each crémeux. Cover with cling film and freeze until firm (about 2 hours).

To make the rocher glaze
Melt the milk chocolate in a heatproof bowl over a pan of barely simmering water. Remove the bowl from the heat, add the oil and stir until smooth. Cool the glaze to 27°C before use.

To finish the assembly
Remove the cakes from the moulds and dip the top half of each into the glaze to cover the crémeux. Remove any excess drips before the glaze sets. Leave the cakes in the fridge to defrost fully, then serve lightly dusted with cocoa, with a chocolate curl on top to decorate, if you wish.

UNASHAMEDLY PISTACHIO

MAKES 8

For the orange blossom syrup
50g water
50g light brown soft sugar
200g orange blossom water

For the pistachio cakes
265g eggs, lightly beaten
100g light brown soft sugar
80g clear honey or liquid glucose
105g finely ground pistachios
110g pistachio paste
155g 35%-fat cream or whipping cream
75g unsalted butter, melted
160g T45 or 00 flour
7g baking powder
a pinch of salt

For the orange blossom crémeux
170g whole milk
170g 35%-fat cream or whipping cream
65g egg yolks
350g 35% white chocolate (such as Valrhona Ivoire), chopped
35g cocoa butter
25g gelatine mass (see page 207)
3 tablespoons orange blossom water, or to taste

For the pistachio glaze
150g 35% white chocolate (such as Valrhona Ivoire), chopped
25g canola oil
240g shelled pistachios

You will also need
Eight 10cm round silicone moulds, 3cm deep
Piping bag fitted with a 1cm plain nozzle

To make the orange blossom syrup
Combine the water with the sugar in a small saucepan and place over a low–medium heat. Leave the sugar to dissolve, then bring the liquid to a boil and immediately remove the pan from the heat. Add the orange blossom water and leave to cool.

To make the pistachio cakes
Heat the oven to 180°C fan.

In a bowl, whisk together the eggs, sugar and honey or glucose. Add the ground pistachios and mix until smooth. Stir in the pistachio paste, cream and butter, then sift in the flour, baking powder and salt, and mix until smooth and combined. You can bake the batter immediately, or cover the bowl and refrigerate overnight.

Weigh 130g of the cake mixture into each mould and bake the cakes for 10 minutes. Reduce the oven temperature to 150°C fan and bake for a further 10 minutes, until well risen and a skewer inserted into the middle of each cake comes out clean. Remove the cakes from the moulds and brush them liberally with orange blossom syrup. Leave to cool, then slice off the domed tops.

To make the orange blossom crémeux
Heat the milk and cream in a small saucepan over a low–medium heat to just below boiling. In a bowl, whisk the egg yolks until they are slightly paler. Gradually pour the hot milk into the bowl, whisking continuously until the mixture is smooth.

Return the mixture to the pan and cook over a low heat, stirring continuously, until thickened and the sauce reaches 80–84°C. Strain the sauce into a clean bowl and leave it to cool slightly.

Partially melt the white chocolate (some molten, some firm) and cocoa butter in a heatproof bowl over a pan of barely simmering water. Using a spatula, mix in the sauce to emulsify. Add the gelatine mass, and the orange blossom water to taste. Blitz with a hand blender until smooth, cover, then refrigerate until firm (about 5 hours).

To begin the assembly
Scoop the crémeux into the piping bag fitted with a 1cm nozzle. Pipe 100g of crémeux into each clean mould, gently press a cake into the crémeux and freeze until firm (about 2 hours).

To make the pistachio glaze
Melt the white chocolate and the oil together in a heatproof bowl set over a pan of barely simmering water. Stir until smooth, then remove from the heat. Cool the glaze to 27°C before using.

To assemble
Unmould the cakes and dip the crémeux layer into the cooled glaze to coat, allowing the excess to drip off. Top each cake with a few shelled pistachios, then refrigerate to fully defrost before serving.

MINCE PIES

MAKES 12

For the mincemeat
100g brandy-macerated currants
100g brandy-macerated sultanas
100g brandy-macerated raisins
20g confit orange or finely chopped candied orange peel
20g confit ginger or finely chopped candied ginger
15g ground mixed spice
5g finely grated orange zest
5g finely grated lemon zest
20g ground almonds

For the almond sablé
90g unsalted butter, at room temperature
70g icing sugar, sifted
40g eggs, lightly beaten
25g ground almonds
180g T45 or 00 flour, sifted
a pinch of salt

For the almond cream
110g unsalted butter, at room temperature
50g dark muscovado sugar
50g eggs, lightly beaten
110g ground almonds
55g cornflour
9g ground mixed spice
a pinch of salt

You will also need
5cm round cutter
4cm round cutter
Piping bag fitted with a 1cm plain nozzle
12-hole non-stick muffin tin (4cm base; 5cm rim)

Every year, our hotels produce thousands of mince pies – this is The Langham's version of the classic. Enjoy them on the day of baking, ideally warm, with a slice of blue cheese on top for an indulgent twist.

To make the mincemeat
Mix all the ingredients together in a bowl. Cover and set aside until you're ready to assemble the pies. This makes more than you need for one batch but it will keep in an airtight box for up to 6 months.

To make the almond sablé
In a mixing bowl, combine the butter and icing sugar and beat until smooth and light. Add the eggs, almonds, flour and salt and mix again until incorporated and smooth.

Roll out the dough between two sheets of baking paper to 2mm thick. Place the sablé on a baking sheet and freeze for 1 hour until firm.

Using the cutters, cut the firm sablé dough into twelve 5cm discs and twelve 4cm discs. If necessary, gather the off-cuts into a ball, re-roll, chill and stamp out more discs. Arrange the discs on two large baking sheets each lined with baking paper.

Chill the discs for 20 minutes. Meanwhile, heat the oven to 160°C fan.

Bake the chilled discs for 10–12 minutes, until firm and the edges are turning golden. Leave to cool while you prepare the almond cream.

To make the almond cream
In a stand mixer fitted with the paddle, cream the butter and sugar for 2 minutes on medium speed until pale and light. Add the eggs and mix again to combine. Stir in the remaining ingredients, mixing until the mixture is smooth. Spoon the mixture into the piping bag fitted with a 1cm nozzle.

To assemble and bake the pies
Place one baked 4cm sablé disc in the bottom of each hollow in your muffin tin. Using two-thirds of the almond cream, pipe equal amounts on top of each disc.

Spoon 10g (about 2 teaspoons) of the mincemeat on to each layer of almond cream and pipe the remaining almond cream over the mincemeat to cover. Press the 5cm discs on top. You can bake the pies immediately; or cover them and freeze them to bake another time.

Heat the oven to 160°C fan.

Bake the pies for about 25 minutes, until golden brown. Leave to cool slightly, then remove them from the moulds. Dust with more icing sugar and serve warm.

LEMON MERINGUE

MAKES 6

For the French meringue kisses
100g egg whites
a pinch of salt
100g caster sugar
50g icing sugar, sifted

For the lemon cream
200g eggs, lightly beaten
185g caster sugar
6g finely grated lemon zest, plus extra (or use lime) to decorate
165g lemon juice
300g unsalted butter, cubed at room temperature

For the pain de genes
350g almond paste (50–52%)
16g finely grated lemon zest
350g eggs, lightly beaten
65g T45 or 00 flour
5g baking powder
110g unsalted butter, melted

For the lemon glaze
125g caster sugar
20g pectin NH
500g water
100g liquid glucose
20g lemon purée or 4 teaspoons lemon juice

You will also need
Piping bag fitted with a 5mm plain nozzle
Six 10cm round silicone moulds, 3cm deep

We love the different textures in this lemon meringue pie. Sometimes we blow torch the meringue at the table – a piece of culinary theatre that not only turns the meringue from white to a caramelised golden brown but also sends the sweet, irresistible aroma of crystallised sugar across the dining room.

To make the French meringue kisses
Heat the oven to 100°C fan. Line two or three large baking sheets with baking paper.

In a stand mixer fitted with the whisk, whisk the egg whites with the salt on medium speed until they hold soft peaks. Little by little, add the caster sugar, whisking until the sugar is completely incorporated and until the meringue holds stiff peaks.

Using a large spoon, one third at a time, fold in the sifted icing sugar, but take care not to over-mix. Scoop the meringue into the piping bag fitted with the 5mm nozzle and pipe thirty-six 2cm kisses on the lined baking sheets, spacing them evenly apart. Bake for about 1 hour or until crisp and dry.

To make the lemon cream
Combine the eggs, sugar, lemon zest and lemon juice in a heatproof bowl and set the bowl over a pan of barely simmering water. Whisking continuously, cook the mixture to 85°C – it should thicken and hold a firm ribbon trail when you lift the whisk.

Remove the bowl from the heat and leave the mixture to cool to 45°C.

Add the butter to the lemon mixture and mix until smooth. Leave to cool, then cover and chill until needed, or for up to 4 days.

To make the pain de genes
Heat the oven to 170°C fan.

Dice the almond paste and tip it into a stand mixer fitted with the paddle. Add the lemon zest and mix on medium speed for about 1 minute to soften.

Change to the whisk attachment and, little by little, add the eggs, mixing well on medium speed between each addition. Continue whisking until the mixture holds a ribbon trail when you lift the whisk.

Sift the flour and baking powder into the bowl and fold them in using a large metal spoon. Add the melted butter and fold until incorporated and no streaks remain.

Spoon 150g of the mixture into each mould and bake for 13–15 minutes, until golden and well risen and a skewer inserted into the centre of each cake comes out clean. Leave the cakes to cool for a few minutes, then remove them from the moulds and transfer them to a wire rack to cool completely.

Continues overleaf

LEMON MERINGUE *CONTINUED*

Cover the top of each cake with 150g of the lemon cream, spreading it into a neat, smooth dome. Freeze the cakes for 2 hours before glazing.

To make the lemon glaze
In a small bowl, mix together the sugar and pectin. Set aside.

Heat the water and the glucose in a small saucepan over a medium heat to 40°C. Add the pectin mixture, stir to combine, then bring to a boil. Boil for 10 seconds, then add the lemon purée or juice and remove the pan from the heat. Leave the glaze to cool to room temperature.

To assemble
One frozen cake at a time, dip the lemon cream into the glaze, allowing any excess to drip off. Transfer the cakes to the fridge and leave the glaze to set (during which time the cakes will also defrost).

Arrange 6 meringue kisses on top of each cake and decorate with finely grated lemon or lime zest to serve.

LANGHAM
LONDON

CHOCOLATE MOUSSE IN A GLASS

MAKES 8

For the chocolate mousse
125g whole milk
125g 35%-fat cream or whipping cream
18g gelatine mass (see page 207)
270g 70% dark chocolate (such as Valrhona Guanaja), chopped
210g pasteurised egg whites
60g caster sugar
a pinch of salt
cocoa powder, for dusting
edible gold leaf, to decorate

For the cinnamon whipped cream
200g 35%-fat cream or whipping cream
25g caster sugar
1g ground cinnamon

You will also need
Piping bag fitted with a 5mm plain nozzle

Adding a delicate cinnamon cream to this light, rich chocolate mousse seriously ups the indulgent factor, elevating the mousse to a level befitting of our Afternoon Tea.

To make the chocolate mousse
In a small saucepan, heat the milk and cream together to 60°C. Remove from the heat, add the gelatine mass, whisk to melt.

In another bowl, partially melt the dark chocolate (some molten, some firm) in a heatproof bowl set over a pan of barely simmering water. Stirring slowly, add the warm cream mixture and mix to combine. Using hand blender, blitz the mixture to a perfect emulsion. Leave to cool to 39°C.

Meanwhile, using a stand mixer, whisk the egg whites, caster sugar and salt into a soft-peak meringue.

Using a large metal spoon, fold one quarter of the meringue into the chocolate mixture to lighten, then fold in the remainder.

Divide the mousse equally between your serving glasses and, using a palette knife, smooth the tops. Cover and chill for at least 2 hours to set.

To make the cinnamon whipped cream
In a mixing bowl, combine all the whipped-cream ingredients and whisk until the mixture holds soft peaks. Scoop the cream into the piping bag fitted with a 5mm plain nozzle and chill until needed. (Or, you can use a spoon for the cream.)

To assemble
Pipe (or spoon) the whipped cinnamon cream on top of each mousse and dust with cocoa powder to serve. Decorate with piece of edible gold leaf, if you wish.

CHAPTER FOUR

BISCUITS

HAZELNUT SOFT COOKIES

MAKES 20

For the praline
100g caster sugar
100g blanched hazelnuts

For the cookies
160g unsalted butter, softened
240g light brown soft sugar
40g dark brown soft sugar
75g eggs, lightly beaten
320g T55 flour or plain flour
8g sea salt
3g bicarbonate of soda
150g hazelnuts, roughly chopped
100g 40% milk chocolate (such as Valrhona Jivara), finely chopped
100g caramel sauce (see page 206), to decorate

You will also need
Piping bag fitted with a 5mm plain nozzle

This extra-hazelnutty cookie positively sings with the flavour of the roasted nuts. Paired with caramel and milk chocolate, it is rich, savoury and perfect with a cup of slightly bitter tea, such an English Breakfast.

To make the praline
Tip the sugar into a small saucepan over a low–medium heat. Leave, without stirring, until it melts. When it starts to caramelise, swirl the pan to ensure an even colour. Once the caramel is a pale toffee colour, add the hazelnuts. Stir to coat, then cook until the caramel has become a deep amber colour. Remove the pan from the heat and turn out the mixture on to a sheet of baking paper. Leave to cool and harden.

Break the hardened praline into pieces. Tip the pieces into a food processor, blitz until smooth, scoop into a bowl, cover and chill until needed (up to 4–5 days).

To make the cookies
In a stand mixer fitted with the paddle, cream the butter and both sugars on medium speed for 2–3 minutes, until creamy and light. Add the eggs and 50g of the hazelnut praline and mix again to combine.

Sift the flour, sea salt and bicarbonate of soda into the bowl, add 100g of the chopped hazelnuts, then the milk chocolate and mix to a well-combined dough.

Line two large baking sheets with baking paper.

Weigh the dough into 20g pieces (you should get 20 cookies altogether), roll each piece into a ball, then flatten it a little. Spoon 5g of the hazelnut praline into the middle of each cookie and gather the dough around the filling. Seal the edges to enclose. Sprinkle a few extra chopped hazelnuts on to the top of each cookie ball and arrange the balls on the lined baking sheets, leaving a little space in between each ball. Refrigerate for 20 minutes while you heat the oven to 170°C fan.

Bake the cookies for 12 minutes, until puffy and starting to firm on top. Remove the baking sheets from the oven (leave the oven on) and press a fish slice on to the top of each cookie to flatten it and crack it slightly. Return the baking sheets to the oven and bake the cookies for a further 2–4 minutes, until the cookies are golden brown.

Leave the cookies to cool completely on the baking sheets. The undecorated cookies will keep in an airtight container for 3–4 days.

To assemble
Immediately before serving, spoon the caramel sauce into the piping bag fitted with a 5mm plain nozzle and pipe dots of caramel sauce over the top of each cookie.

VANILLA BISCUITS

MAKES 30

160g unsalted butter, softened
75g caster sugar, plus 20g extra for sprinkling
seeds from ¼ vanilla bean
a pinch of salt
230g T45 or 00 flour

You will also need
4.5cm plain round cutter

Typically, vanilla biscuits are rolled into logs, sliced and baked. However, we roll out the dough flat, so that we can use a round cutter to give them a uniform look. At The Langham we use fragrant Tahitian vanilla to gently spice our biscuits, but you can swap in any spice you prefer.

In a stand mixer fitted with the paddle, cream together the butter, sugar, vanilla seeds and salt for about 3 minutes on medium speed until pale and light.

Sift the flour into the bowl and mix again on low speed to a well-combined dough. Shape the dough into a ball, then flatten the ball into a disc, cover and chill for about 30 minutes to firm up.

Place a large sheet of baking paper on your work surface and the dough disc on top. Place another sheet on top of that. Roll out the dough between the two sheets until 8mm thick. Transfer to the fridge and chill again for 30 minutes, until firm.

Meanwhile, heat the oven to 140°C fan. Line a large baking sheet with baking paper.

Using the 4.5cm plain round cutter, stamp out 30 discs (each weighing about 15g), gathering the off-cuts and re-rolling as necessary. Arrange the discs on lined baking sheets. Sprinkle the biscuits evenly with the extra caster sugar, then bake them for 15–18 minutes, until firm and pale golden.

Leave the biscuits to cool on the baking sheets. They will keep in an airtight container for up to 3–4 days.

GANACHE-FILLED SABLÉ BISCUITS

MAKES 24

For the almond sablé biscuits
90g unsalted butter, softened
70g icing sugar, sifted
a pinch of salt
40g eggs, lightly beaten
170g ground almonds
185g T45 or 00 flour

For the chocolate ganache
120g 35%-fat cream or whipping cream
30g liquid glucose
130g 70% dark chocolate (such as Valrhona Nyangbo), finely chopped
15g unsalted butter, cubed

You will also need
4.5cm plain round cutter
Piping bag fitted with a 5mm plain nozzle

To make the almond sablé biscuits
In a stand mixer fitted with the paddle, cream the butter with the icing sugar and salt for about 3 minutes on medium speed until creamy and light.

Add the eggs and mix to combine. Add the ground almonds and flour and slowly mix again until smooth. Flatten the dough into a disc, then cover it and chill it for 30 minutes to firm up.

Line 2–3 large baking sheets with baking paper (or bake in batches if you don't have enough baking sheets).

Lay a large sheet of baking paper on your work surface and place the sablé dough on top. Top with another sheet of baking paper. Roll out the sablé between the two sheets until 2–3mm thick. Using the 4.5cm plain round cutter, stamp out 48 discs (each should weigh 23g), re-rolling the trimmings as necessary. Arrange the discs on the lined baking sheets, spacing them slightly apart. Chill them while you heat the oven to 140°C fan.

Bake the chilled sablé discs for about 20 minutes, until pale golden.

To make the ganache
In a small saucepan, heat the cream and glucose to 80°C.

Melt the chocolate to 45°C either in a heatproof bowl set over a pan of barely simmering water. Add half of the hot cream to the chocolate and, using a spatula, mix well to combine.

Remove the bowl from the heat and add the rest of the cream. Use a hand blender to blitz the mixture to a perfect emulsion.

Leave the ganache to cool to 35–40°C, then add the diced butter and use a hand blender again to blitz to a perfect emulsion. Scoop the ganache into the piping bag fitted with a 5mm plain nozzle and leave it at 18°C (cool room temperature) to set for at least 24 hours before use.

To assemble
Turn half of the sablés flat side uppermost and pipe 15g of the ganache on top of each upturned surface. Lightly press another sablé biscuit, flat side downwards, on top to sandwich the ganache. The filled biscuits will keep in an airtight container for 2–3 days.

PECAN, COFFEE AND CHOCOLATE VEGAN COOKIES

MAKES 14

100g unsalted plant-based butter
70g caster sugar
70g light brown soft sugar
50g liquid egg replacement
210g gluten-free plain flour
½ teaspoon xanthan gum
5g baking powder
5g coffee powder
a pinch of salt
150g 70% vegan dark chocolate chips
60g caramelised pecan nuts, chopped

We bake these cookies so that the chocolate chunks are just melted and the cookie has a soft texture – best enjoyed straight from the oven. If you prefer your cookies firmer, with a crispy texture, bake them for a minute or two longer.

In a stand mixer fitted with the paddle, cream together the butter and both sugars on medium speed for about 3 minutes, until pale and light.

Add the liquid egg replacement and mix again.

Sift the flour, xanthan gum, baking powder, coffee powder and salt into the bowl, then add the chocolate chips and pecans. Mix to a well-combined dough.

Line two large baking sheets with baking paper.

Weigh the dough into 50g pieces and shape each piece into a ball (you should get 14 cookies altogether). Arrange the balls on lined baking sheets. Refrigerate for 20 minutes while you heat the oven to 170°C fan.

Bake the cookies for about 14 minutes, until puffy and starting to turn golden at the edges. Remove the baking sheets from the oven (leave the oven on) and press a fish slice on to the top of each cookie to flatten it and crack it slightly. Return the baking sheets to the oven and bake the cookies for a further 1 minute until the top is set and the edges are firm.

Leave the cookies to cool completely on the baking sheets. They will keep in an airtight container for 3–4 days.

MATCHA CRANBERRY COOKIES

MAKES 24

190g unsalted butter, softened
270g caster sugar
100g eggs, lightly beaten
400g T45 or 00 flour
10g baking powder
a big pinch of salt
25g ceremonial-grade matcha powder
150g white chocolate chips (such as Valrhona Ivoire)
70g cranberries

In a stand mixer fitted with the paddle, cream the butter and sugar on medium speed for about 3 minutes, until creamy and light.

Add the beaten eggs and mix until smooth.

Sift the flour, baking powder and salt into the bowl, then stir in the matcha, chocolate chips and cranberries and mix again to a well-combined dough.

Line two large baking sheets with baking paper.

Weigh the dough into 50g pieces and roll each piece into a ball (you should get 24 cookies altogether). Place the balls on the lined baking sheets, spaced well apart. Refrigerate for 30–60 minutes while you heat the oven to 170°C fan.

Bake the chilled cookies for about 12 minutes, until puffy and starting to firm on top. Remove the sheets from the oven (but leave the oven on) and press a fish slice on to the top of each cookie to flatten it and crack it slightly. Return the baking sheets to the oven and bake the cookies for a further 2 minutes, until the top is set and the edges are firm.

Leave the cookies to cool completely on the baking sheets. They will keep in an airtight container for 3–4 days.

LANGHAM PINK COOKIES

MAKES 20

145g unsalted butter, softened
200g caster sugar
75g eggs, lightly beaten
red food-colouring paste or gel
310g T45 or 00 flour
8g baking powder
50g desiccated coconut
225g white chocolate chips (such as Valrhona Ivoire)
8g freeze-dried raspberry powder
4g salt

These well-loved cookies are an absolute classic in The Langham hotels around the world. Not only are they Langham pink, but the raspberry, white chocolate and coconut flavours match superbly well to give a distinctive flavour, too.

In a stand mixer fitted with the paddle, cream the butter and sugar on medium speed for about 3 minutes, until creamy and light.

Add the egg and a little red food colouring and mix until smooth and you have an even pink colour.

Sift the flour and baking powder into the bowl. Add the coconut, chocolate chips, freeze-dried raspberry powder and salt. Mix again on low speed until you have a well-combined dough.

Line two large baking sheets with baking paper.

Weigh the dough into 50g pieces and roll each piece into a ball (you should get 20 cookies altogether). Place the balls on the lined baking sheets, spaced well apart. Refrigerate for 30 minutes while you heat the oven to 160°C fan.

Bake the chilled cookies for about 12 minutes, until puffy and starting to firm on top. Remove the sheets from the oven (but leave the oven on) and press a fish slice on to the top of each cookie to flatten it and crack it slightly. Return the baking sheets to the oven and bake the cookies for a further 1 minute, until the top is set and the edges are firm.

Leave the cookies to cool completely on the baking sheets. They will keep in an airtight container for 3–4 days.

DOUBLE DARK CHOCOLATE COOKIES

MAKES 12

100g unsalted butter, softened
135g dark brown soft sugar
50g eggs, lightly beaten
170g T45 or 00 flour
35g cocoa powder
5g baking powder
½ teaspoon salt
150g 66% dark chocolate chips (such as Valrhona Caraïbe)

Can you ever have enough chocolate? Chunks of dark, melted chocolate are held together with a cocoa dough. We serve these warm, just out of the oven.

In a stand mixer fitted with the paddle, cream the butter and sugar together for 2–3 minutes on medium speed until creamy and light.

Add the eggs and mix again to combine.

Sift the flour, cocoa, baking powder and salt into the bowl, add the chocolate chips and mix again on low speed until the mixture forms a well-combined dough.

Line two large baking sheets with baking paper.

Weigh the dough into 50g pieces and roll each piece into a ball (you should get 12 cookies altogether). Place the balls on the lined baking sheets, spaced well apart. Refrigerate for 30 minutes while you heat the oven to 170°C fan.

Bake the chilled cookies for about 12 minutes, until puffy and starting to firm on top. Remove the sheets from the oven (but leave the oven on) and press a fish slice on to the top of each cookie to flatten it and crack it slightly. Return the baking sheets to the oven and bake the cookies for a further 2 minutes, until the top is set and the edges are firm.

Leave the cookies to cool completely on the baking sheets. They will keep in an airtight container for 3–4 days.

SEA-SALT CHOCOLATE CHIP BISCUITS

MAKES 30

105g unsalted butter, softened
65g light brown soft sugar
25g caster sugar
155g T55 or plain flour
25g cocoa powder
2g bicarbonate of soda
a pinch of salt
90g 70% chocolate chips (such as Valrhona Guanaja), chopped to a rubble
sea-salt flakes

You will also need
4.5cm plain round cutter

In a stand mixer fitted with the paddle, cream the butter and both sugars together for about 3 minutes on medium speed until creamy and light.

Sift the flour, cocoa powder, bicarbonate of soda and salt into the bowl and mix to a well-combined dough.

Add the chopped chocolate chips and mix again to combine. Knead the dough by hand for 1 minute to bring it together.

Line two large baking sheets with baking paper.

Flatten the dough ball into a disc. Place a large sheet of baking paper on your work surface, top it with the dough disc and place another sheet of baking paper on top. Roll the dough between the two sheets until 8mm thick. Using the 4.5cm plain round cutter, stamp out 30 discs (each should weigh 15g). Gather the off-cuts and re-roll the dough as necessary. Arrange the discs on the lined baking sheets. Refrigerate for 20 minutes while you heat the oven to 140°C fan.

Sprinkle sea-salt flakes over each biscuit, according to your preference, then bake for 15–18 minutes, until crisp.

Leave the biscuits to cool completely on the baking sheets. They will keep in an airtight container for 3–4 days.

CURRY AND SESAME BISCUITS

MAKES 30

135g unsalted butter, softened
100g caster sugar
a pinch of salt
25g egg yolks, lightly beaten
175g T55 or 00 flour, plus extra for rolling
10g curry powder
15g black sesame seeds, plus extra for sprinkling
5g white sesame seeds, plus extra for sprinkling
20g flaked almonds

You will also need
4.5cm plain round cutter

Not all the biscuits in our Afternoon Tea are of the sweet kind. These savoury, curry-spiced bites pack a sweet-salty punch, with a sprinkle of sesame for an extra pop of texture. They are delicious just as they come, spread with butter, or alongside your favourite artisan cheeses.

In a stand mixer fitted with the paddle, cream the butter, sugar and salt together for about 3 minutes on medium speed until creamy and light.

Add the egg yolks and mix to combine.

Sift the flour and curry powder into the bowl, add both sesame seeds and the flaked almonds and mix until it all comes together to form a well-combined dough. Flatten the dough into a disc, then cover it and chill it for 30 minutes.

Line two large baking sheets with baking paper.

On a lightly floured surface roll out the chilled dough until 8mm thick. Using the 4.5cm plain round cutter, stamp out 30 discs (each disc should weigh 15g), re-rolling the trimmings as necessary. In batches if necessary, arrange the discs on the lined baking sheets, spacing them slightly apart. Sprinkle over a few more sesame seeds, then chill for 20 minutes while you heat the oven to 140°C fan.

Bake the chilled biscuits for 15–18 minutes, until golden. Leave the biscuits to cool completely on the baking sheets. They will keep in an airtight container for 3–4 days.

CHAPTER FIVE

SCONES & JAM

THE LANGHAM'S SCONES

MAKES ABOUT 20

450g T45 or 00 flour, plus extra for rolling
17g baking powder
125g unsalted butter, cubed and chilled
125g caster sugar
5g salt
100g eggs, beaten, plus extra for glazing
100g whole milk or buttermilk

You will also need
5cm plain round cutter

The Langham's scones are renowned for being light and fluffy – thanks to a light kneading by hand as soon as the mixture has come together.

In a stand mixer fitted with the paddle, combine the flour, baking powder, butter, sugar and salt and mix on low speed to rub the butter into the dry ingredients to a fine, grainy texture (about 3 minutes). Add the beaten eggs and milk or buttermilk and mix until combined.

Turn out the dough on to your work surface and knead for about 1 minute, until smooth.

On a lightly floured sheet of baking paper, roll out the dough to a circle 2.5cm thick. Using the baking paper, slide the dough on to a baking sheet. Loosely cover, then chill for 10–20 minutes in the fridge while you heat the oven to 180°C fan.

Line two large baking sheets with baking paper.

Dust the 5cm plain round cutter with flour and stamp out rounds from the dough. Arrange the rounds on the lined baking sheets, leaving a 5cm gap between each one. Gather the offcuts together into a ball, re-roll once and stamp out more scones. You should get about 20 altogether.

Brush the top of the scones with a little extra beaten egg and bake for about 20 minutes, until risen and golden brown.

EARL GREY SULTANA SCONES

MAKES ABOUT 25

7g Earl Grey tea leaves
75g freshly boiled water
140g sultanas
450g T45 or 00 flour, plus extra for rolling
17g baking powder
125g unsalted butter, cubed and chilled
125g caster sugar
5g salt
100g eggs, beaten, plus extra for glazing
75–100g whole milk or buttermilk

You will also need
5cm plain round cutter

Tip the tea leaves into a bowl and pour over the boiled water. Leave the tea to infuse for 5 minutes, then strain it into a clean bowl and add the sultanas. Stir well to combine and leave to cool, stirring from time to time. Cover and leave overnight at room temperature to soak.

In a stand mixer fitted with the paddle, combine the flour, baking powder, butter, sugar and salt and mix on low speed to rub the butter into the dry ingredients to a fine, grainy texture (about 3 minutes). Add the beaten eggs, milk or buttermilk and soaked sultanas and mix until combined.

Turn out the dough on to your work surface and knead for about 1 minute, until smooth.

On a lightly floured sheet of baking paper, roll out the dough to a circle 2.5cm thick. Using the baking paper, slide the dough on to a baking sheet. Loosely cover, then chill for 10–20 minutes in the fridge while you heat the oven to 180°C fan.

Line two large baking sheets with baking paper.

Dust the 5cm plain round cutter with flour and stamp out rounds from the dough. Arrange the rounds on the lined baking sheets, leaving a 5cm gap between each one. Gather the offcuts together into a ball, re-roll once and stamp out more scones. You should get about 25 altogether.

Brush the top of the scones with a little extra beaten egg and bake for about 20 minutes, until risen and golden brown.

CHEESE SCONES

MAKES ABOUT 30

450g T45 or 00 flour,
plus extra for rolling
20g baking powder
125g unsalted butter,
chilled and diced
75g parmesan, finely grated,
plus extra for sprinkling
5g salt
130g eggs, beaten,
plus extra for glazing
135g whole milk
75g Cheddar,
finely chopped

Warm from the oven, broken open and topped with a spoonful of butter that melts in the heat of the scone, these airy, savoury versions of our sweet classic are decidedly moreish. Salted butter and tomato chutney (see page 187) make a delicious and simple topping. A slice of tangy blue cheese would be good, too.

In a stand mixer fitted with the paddle, combine the flour, baking powder, butter, parmesan and salt and mix on low speed to rub the butter into the dry ingredients to a fine, grainy texture. Add the beaten eggs, milk and Cheddar and mix again on low speed until combined.

Turn out the dough on to your work surface and knead for about 1 minute, until smooth.

On a lightly floured sheet of baking paper, roll out the dough to a rectangle 1.5cm thick (the rectangle should be about 22cm x 19cm). Using the baking paper, slide the dough on to a baking sheet. Loosely cover, then chill for 10–20 minutes in the fridge while you heat the oven to 180°C fan.

Trim the edges of the dough to make a rectangle 21cm x 18cm, and cut the scones into 3.5cm squares (making 6 along the long edge and 5 along the short edge, to give 30 squares altogether). Brush the scones with extra beaten egg to glaze and sprinkle with extra parmesan. Bake the scones for about 18 minutes, until risen and golden brown.

STRAWBERRY JAM

MAKES ABOUT 1.8KG

1.2kg strawberries, hulled and quartered
1kg caster sugar
8g powdered pectin
20g lemon juice

The Langham's strawberry jam is less sweet than the norm to allow the freshness of the fruit to shine through and to preserve its vibrant colour. The method here means it cooks really quickly – especially if you use as big a saucepan as you can find.

Start by sterilising the jars. Heat the oven to 110°C. Wash the jars in hot soapy water and rinse well. Place the jars on a baking tray and place them in the warm oven for at least 10 minutes – or the time it takes to make the jam. Wash the lids, place them in a pan of water, bring to a boil and simmer for 5 minutes. Remove the pan from the heat but leave the lids in the water until needed.

Weigh the prepared strawberries – you will need 1kg prepped weight. Tip the strawberries and half of the sugar into a large saucepan and place over a low heat. Stir often for about 12 minutes to soften the berries and dissolve the sugar.

In a bowl, mix the remaining sugar with the pectin. Add this to the pan with the lemon juice and bring to a boil over a medium heat. Continue to cook at a rapid boil for about 15 minutes, until the jam reaches a setting point of 105°C on a sugar thermometer. While the jam is boiling, use a spoon to remove any scum that rises to the top.

Once the jam reaches setting point, remove the pan from the heat and leave the jam to settle for 5 minutes. Pour it into the sterilised jars and seal immediately with dry lids. Label the jars once the jam is cold.

Pasteurising Jams and Marmalades
If you wish to pasteurise your jam or marmalade, fill the sterilised jars with the jam or marmalade while it is still molten and hot, straight from the pan. Cover each jar with a dry lid and tightly seal. Place the jars in a large saucepan with a steamer basket, or place a folded tea towel in the bottom of the pan and place the jars on top – whichever method you use, make sure that the jars do not touch. Fill the pan with water to cover the jars by 3–4cm. Place the pan on the hob and bring the water to a boil over a medium heat. Reduce the heat to a simmer and cook for 15–20 minutes.

Remove the pan from the heat and leave the jars to cool for 15 minutes, then carefully remove them from the pan and place them upside down on a clean tea towel until the contents are completely cold.

FIG AND SPICE JAM

MAKES ABOUT 625G

550g Provence or purple figs, trimmed and roughly chopped
1 small cinnamon stick
1 star anise
seeds from ⅛ of a vanilla bean
a pinch of freshly ground black pepper
260g caster sugar
20g lemon juice
30g water

Start by sterilising the jars. Heat the oven to 110°C. Wash the jars in hot soapy water and rinse well. Place the jars on a baking tray and place them in the warm oven for at least 10 minutes – or the time it takes to make the jam. Wash the lids, place them in a pan of water, bring to a boil and simmer for 5 minutes. Remove the pan from the heat but leave the lids in the water until needed.

Tip the figs into a large saucepan and add the spices, caster sugar, lemon juice and water. Mix to combine, cover and set aside at room temperature for 30 minutes, until the figs are soft and very juicy.

Place the pan on a medium heat and bring the liquid to a boil. Cook, stirring often for about 15 minutes, until the fruit is very soft and the jam thickened, and has reached a setting point of 105°C on a sugar thermometer.

Once the jam has reached setting point, remove the pan from the heat and leave the jam to settle for 5 minutes. Pour it into your sterilised jars and seal immediately with dry lids. Label the jars once the jam is cold.

THE LANGHAM

PINEAPPLE JAM

MAKES ABOUT 1.4KG

1kg peeled and cored fresh pineapple
750g caster sugar
30g freshly grated ginger
20g lemon or lime juice
8g powdered pectin

Start by sterilising the jars. Heat the oven to 110°C. Wash the jars in hot soapy water and rinse well. Place the jars on a baking tray and place them in the warm oven for at least 10 minutes – or the time it takes to make the jam. Wash the lids, place them in a pan of water, bring to a boil and simmer for 5 minutes. Remove the pan from the heat but leave the lids in the water until needed.

Chop the prepared pineapple into 1cm pieces – either by hand or pulse them in a food processor. Tip the pineapple into a large saucepan, add half of the sugar, the ginger and the lemon juice and mix to combine.

Set the pan over a low heat and cook, stirring often, for about 15 minutes, until the sugar has dissolved and the pineapple is softened and juicy.

In a bowl mix the remaining sugar with the pectin and add them to the pan. Increase the heat to medium, stir to dissolve the sugar and bring to a boil. Cook at a rapid boil for about 10 minutes, until the jam reaches a setting point of 105°C on a sugar thermometer.

Once the jam has reached setting point, remove the pan from the heat and leave the jam to settle for 5 minutes. Pour it into your sterilised jars and seal immediately with dry lids. Label the jars once the jam is cold.

MANDARIN MARMALADE

MAKES ABOUT 2KG

1.5kg mandarins
1.5kg caster sugar
20g lemon juice

This marmalade uses the whole fruit, managing to preserve that tangy, fresh mandarin acidity even after cooking.

Wash the mandarins in hot soapy water, rinse, then slice off the stalks. Place the fruit in a large saucepan, cover with water and poach over a low–medium heat for about 40 minutes, until soft.

Drain and leave the fruit in a colander for 30 minutes to remove as much excess water as possible.

Cut the mandarins into quarters and remove any pips. Tip the fruit into a food processor and pulse to chop into 1cm pieces. Tip the pieces into a large saucepan or preserving pan and add the sugar. Place over a low heat and stir occasionally to dissolve the sugar. Once the sugar has dissolved, increase the heat to medium and bring to a boil. Cook at a steady boil for about 30 minutes, stirring often to prevent the marmalade catching on the bottom of the pan. When the marmalade reaches a setting point of 105°C on a sugar thermometer, add the lemon juice and remove the pan from the heat.

Meanwhile sterilise the jars. Heat the oven to 110°C. Wash the jars in hot soapy water and rinse well. Place the jars on a baking tray and place them in the warm oven for at least 10 minutes – or the time it takes to make the marmalade. Wash the lids, place them in a pan of water, bring to a boil and simmer for 5 minutes. Remove the pan from the heat but leave the lids in the water until needed.

Once the marmalade is ready, leave it to settle in the pan for 5 minutes. Then, pour it into the sterilised jars and seal immediately with dry lids. Label the jars once the marmalade is cold.

RASPBERRY JAM

MAKES ABOUT 1.8KG

1kg raspberries
1kg caster sugar
6 drops of rose essence
4g powdered pectin
10g lemon juice
15g food-grade dried rose petals

Start by sterilising the jars. Heat the oven to 110°C. Wash the jars in hot soapy water and rinse well. Place the jars on a baking tray and place them in the warm oven for at least 10 minutes – or the time it takes to make the jam. Wash the lids, place them in a pan of water, bring to a boil and simmer for 5 minutes. Remove the pan from the heat but leave the lids in the water until needed.

Tip the raspberries, half of the sugar and the rose essence into a large saucepan and place the pan over a low heat. Stir with a wooden spoon to lightly crush the berries. Cook for about 5 minutes to soften the berries and dissolve the sugar.

In a bowl, mix the remaining sugar with the pectin. Add the mixture to the pan with the lemon juice and bring the liquid to a boil over a medium heat. Cook at a rapid boil until the jam reaches a setting point of 105°C on a sugar thermometer. While the jam is boiling, use a spoon to remove any scum that rises to the top.

Once the jam has reached setting point, remove the pan from the heat and leave the jam to settle for 5 minutes, then stir in the rose petals. Pour the jam into your sterilised jars and seal immediately with dry lids. Label the jars once the jam is cold.

SPICED TOMATO CHUTNEY

MAKES 500–550G

1 tablespoon sunflower oil
1kg cherry tomatoes, halved
40g shallots, finely diced
1 garlic clove, crushed
1g thyme leaves (about 1 sprig) or ½ teaspoon dried
1g dried basil
100g caster sugar
100ml apple cider vinegar
2g Espelette pepper or pul biber
salt and freshly ground black pepper

Tomato chutney is the perfect complement to savoury scones (see page 174) or to serve with a cheese course during Afternoon Tea. This one has a delicate spice balanced by the freshness of the dried basil and thyme.

Start by sterilising the jars. Heat the oven to 110°C. Wash the jars in hot soapy water and rinse well. Place the jars on a baking tray and place them in the warm oven for at least 10 minutes – or the time it takes to make the chutney. Wash the lids, place them in a pan of water, bring to a boil and simmer for 5 minutes. Remove the pan from the heat but leave the lids in the water until needed.

Heat the sunflower oil in a large saucepan over a high heat. Add the cherry tomatoes and cook for about 5 minutes, stirring occasionally, until they start to break down.

Add the shallots, garlic, thyme, basil and a generous pinch of salt. Reduce the heat to low–medium and cook for about 5 minutes, allowing the aromatics to soften and blend.

Add the sugar, vinegar and Espelette pepper or pul biber. Bring the mixture to a simmer, then reduce the heat to low. Cook gently for about 30 minutes, stirring often until the mixture thickens to a jammy consistency and begins to slightly caramelise on the bottom of the pan.

Remove the pan from the heat, taste, and adjust the seasoning if needed. Leave the chutney to cool, then pour it into the sterilised jars and seal immediately with dry lids. Label the jars once the chutney is cold.

The tomato chutney will store in the fridge for up to 2 weeks.

CHAPTER SIX

BASICS

Professional

THE LANGHAM MAYONNAISE

MAKES ABOUT 550G

3 egg yolks
1 tablespoon Dijon mustard
7g fine salt, plus extra to taste if necessary
½ teaspoon finely ground white pepper, plus extra to taste if necessary
500ml vegetable oil
½ tablespoon white wine vinegar or lemon juice

A great mayonnaise really ties a sandwich together, delivering an unctuous texture and underlying savouriness. This mayo actually binds the ingredients, making them easily spreadable and elegantly sliceable for our perfect and precise serve.

Combine the egg yolks, mustard, salt and pepper in a bowl and mix with a balloon whisk for about 2 minutes, until pale.

Very slowly and gradually add the oil, whisking continuously as you do so, until the mixture is smooth and thick. Add the vinegar or lemon juice and adjust the seasoning to taste.

The mayo will keep in a clean jar in the fridge for up to 5 days.

ALMOND SABLÉ

MAKES ABOUT 800G

180g unsalted butter,
at room temperature
135g icing sugar, sifted
3g salt
75g eggs, lightly beaten
45g ground almonds
360g T45 or 00 flour

In a stand mixer fitted with the paddle, combine the butter, icing sugar and salt on low speed until thoroughly mixed, smooth and light.

Add the beaten eggs and mix to just combine. Add the ground almonds and flour and mix again until thoroughly combined and smooth.

Flatten the dough into a disc, cover with cling film and chill until needed. Use as instructed in the recipe. Any leftover will freeze well for another time.

SWEET PASTRY

MAKES ABOUT 800G

100g icing sugar
400g T55 or plain flour
45g ground almonds
180g unsalted butter, cubed and chilled
70–75g eggs, lightly beaten

Sift the icing sugar, flour and ground almonds into the bowl of a stand mixer fitted with the paddle. Add the butter and mix on low speed until the butter has been rubbed into the dry ingredients and the mixture is crumbly.

Add the eggs and mix again for 30 seconds until the mixture forms a smooth dough. Flatten the dough into a disc, cover and chill for about 1 hour until firm, or until needed. Use as instructed in the recipe. Any leftover will freeze well for another time.

CHOCOLATE SWEET PASTRY

MAKES ABOUT 800G

100g icing sugar
340g T55 or plain flour
60g cocoa powder
45g ground almonds
180g unsalted butter, chilled and cubed
70g eggs, lightly beaten

Sift the icing sugar, flour, cocoa and ground almonds into the bowl of a stand mixer fitted with the paddle. Add the butter and mix on low speed until the butter has been rubbed into the dry ingredients and the mixture is crumbly.

Add the eggs and mix again for 30 seconds until the mixture forms a smooth dough. Flatten the dough into a disc, cover and chill for about 1 hour until firm, or until needed. Use as instructed in the recipe. Any leftover will freeze well for another time.

INVERTED PUFF PASTRY

MAKES ABOUT 1.4KG

For the detrempe (base dough)
420g T45 or 00 flour, plus extra for dusting
18g salt
135g unsalted butter (84% fat), cubed and chilled
180g water
3g white vinegar

For the beurrage
180g T45 or 00 flour
450g unsalted butter

To make the base dough
Place the flour, salt and butter in a stand mixer fitted with the dough hook and slowly mix everything to loosely combine. Add the water and vinegar and keep mixing for 3 minutes on low speed, then increase the speed to medium and continue mixing for about 10 minutes, until the dough is smooth, elastic and will create a clear windowpane when a little of the dough is stretched between your fingers. Once the dough is ready, flatten it into a neat rectangle.

Wrap the puff pastry and leave it to rest in the fridge overnight. Meanwhile prepare the beurrage.

To make the beurrage
Combine the flour and butter in the stand mixer fitted with the paddle and mix until smooth.

Roll out the beurrage between two sheets of baking paper into a neat rectangle that is of even thickness and is twice as large as the base dough. Leave covered and rest the beurrage in the fridge overnight.

To finish the pastry
Place the beurrage on a floured work surface and place the dough on top in the middle of the beurrage at a 45° angle, so that the corners of the dough sit in the middle of each side of the beurrage. Fold the beurrage around the dough to enclose it completely.

Wrap, and chill again for 20 minutes.

If you're rolling the pastry by hand, flour the work surface and roll out the dough to a long, neat rectangle that is three times as long as it is wide. Fold the top of the rectangle down to the middle to cover the middle third and the bottom third up to cover this. This is a single fold. Wrap, and chill the pastry for 30 minutes.

Repeat this folding and chilling a further 4 times to make a total of 5 single folds. Then, chill the dough for 2 hours or until needed.

If you're using a dough breaker, roll out the dough to a long rectangle, make 5 single folds, wrapping and resting the dough in the fridge for at least 1 hour in between each single fold.

Once the folds are complete and the dough has rested, flour the work surface again and roll the dough to use as needed. Any leftover will freeze well for another time.

CHOUX PASTRY

MAKES ABOUT 900G

For the choux pastry
150g whole milk
150g water
130g unsalted butter, cubed
18g caster sugar
6g salt
180g T55 or plain flour, sifted
290g eggs, lightly beaten

For the craquelin
110g caster sugar
90g unsalted butter, softened
110g T55 or plain flour

You will also need
Piping bag fitted with a 5mm plain nozzle
2cm plain round cutter

This recipe makes about 150 bite-sized choux buns each topped with a craquelin disc. Use a larger nozzle and cutter to make fewer, larger finished buns, then adjust the baking time accordingly.

Pour the milk into a small saucepan, add the water, butter, sugar and salt. Place the pan over a medium heat to melt the butter. Once the butter has melted, bring the liquid to a boil, then immediately remove the pan from the heat.

Add the sifted flour and beat well until smooth and thoroughly incorporated.

Place the pan back over a low heat and stir with a spatula for about 1 minute, until the mixture dries out, is smooth and cleanly leaves the side of the pan.

Scoop the mixture into the bowl of a stand mixer fitted with the paddle and leave to cool for 5 minutes to 40°C.

Gradually add the beaten eggs, mixing continuously on low–medium speed until the mixture is glossy, smooth, reluctantly drops off a spoon and will hold a firm peak.

Cover the bowl and leave the choux pastry to rest at room temperature for 2 hours.

Meanwhile, prepare the craquelin.

To make the craquelin
In a small bowl, beat the sugar, butter and flour together until smooth. Roll out the craquelin dough between two sheets of baking paper until 2mm thick. Place it on a baking sheet and freeze for 30 minutes, until firm.

To assemble and bake the buns
Heat the oven to 170°C fan.

Scoop the choux into the piping bag fitted with a 5mm plain nozzle and pipe approximately 5g mounds on to silicone air mats or on to baking sheets lined with baking paper.

Using the 2cm round cutter, stamp out discs from the frozen craquelin dough and place one on top of each choux mound.

Bake the choux for about 17 minutes, until the buns are golden brown, well risen and crisp. Leave to cool before filling.

TEMPERED CHOCOLATE

Tempering chocolate makes it smooth, glossy, firm and resistant to blooming. Always use good-quality chocolate, such as a couverture, which is richer in cocoa butter (at least 31%) and so easier to handle.

For perfect tempering, whether using dark, milk or white chocolate, you will need to melt the chocolate over a bain marie (there are other methods, but this is the simplest for the home cook) within a specific temperature range. For that reason, you will also need an accurate digital food thermometer.

Unless you are using couverture chocolate drops, chop your chocolate into 1 cm pieces. Tip the chocolate into a heatproof bowl – preferably glass or ceramic – and place the bowl over a pan of barely simmering water. Do not allow the bottom of the bowl to come into contact with the water. Pop the thermometer into the bowl and, stirring often, melt the chocolate. Take care not to allow any water into the bowl.

For dark chocolate, melt it to 50–55°C (122–131°F)
For milk chocolate, melt it to 45–50°C (113–122°F)
For white or dulcey chocolate, melt it to 45–50°C (113–122°F)

Do not allow the temperature of the melted chocolate to rise above the maximum temperature for the type of chocolate you're using.

Once the chocolate has melted to within the temperature range, immediately remove the bowl from the bain marie and sit it in a larger bowl of cold water to cool – again being careful not to allow any water into the chocolate. Using a rubber spatula, stir the chocolate regularly to cool it to 35°C (95°F).

Remove the bowl of chocolate from the cold water, place it on your work surface and continue stirring and cooling to:

For dark chocolate, 28–29°C (82–84°F)
For milk chocolate, 27–28°C (81–82°F)
For white or dulcey chocolate, 26–27°C (79–81°F)

Finally, briefly place the melted chocolate back over the bain marie and warm it to its working temperature:

For dark chocolate, 31–32°C (88–90°F)
For milk chocolate, 29–30°C (84–86°F)
For white or dulcey chocolate, 28–29°C (82–84°F)

The chocolate is now ready to use.

LANGHAM

CHOCOLATE GLAZE

MAKES ABOUT 1.3KG

135g water
460g caster sugar
50g liquid glucose
110g 35%-fat cream
 or whipping cream
25g skimmed milk powder
140g cocoa powder
240g neutral glaze
 (see below)
180g gelatine mass
 (see page 207)

In a small saucepan over a low–medium heat, combine 110g of the water with 110g of the sugar and all the glucose and heat to 40°C.

Add the cream, milk powder, cocoa powder and remaining 350g of sugar and bring to a boil.

In another pan, bring the neutral glaze to a boil over a low–medium heat. Remove from the heat, then add the remaining 25g of water and the gelatine mass. Stir to combine and to melt the gelatine.

Add the gelatine mixture to the cocoa syrup mixture, stir to combine, then leave to cool to room temperature.

Pour the glaze into a clean bowl or food container, cover and refrigerate for 24 hours. Reheat the refrigerated glaze to 33–35°C before using.

NEUTRAL GLAZE

MAKES ABOUT 750G

125g caster sugar
20g pectin NH
500g water
100g liquid glucose
20g lemon juice

In a small bowl, combine the sugar and pectin.

In a saucepan, heat the water and glucose to 40°C. Add the pectin mixture, stir to combine, then bring to a boil. Boil for 10 seconds, then add the lemon juice and remove the pan from the heat.

Pour the glaze into a clean bowl or food container, cover and refrigerate for 12 hours. Reheat the refrigerated glaze to 30–34°C before using.

WHITE CHOCOLATE GLAZE

MAKES ABOUT 850G

85g water
170g caster sugar
160g liquid glucose
55g whole milk
60g condensed milk
90g gelatine mass (see page 207)
85g neutral glaze (see opposite)
170g 33% white chocolate (such as Valrhona Opalys), chopped
fat-soluble food-colouring (as required)

In a small saucepan, combine the water, sugar and glucose and bring to a boil over a low–medium heat, stirring to dissolve the sugar.

Add the milk and condensed milk, stir to combine and return the mixture to a boil.

Remove the pan from the heat, add the gelatine mass and neutral glaze, stir to combine and to melt the gelatine smoothly. Leave to cool to 60°C.

Meanwhile, melt the chocolate in a heatproof bowl over a pan of barely simmering water. Stir until smooth and remove from the heat.

Add the melted chocolate to the milk mixture (and add the food colouring, if using) and use a hand blender to blitz the two together to form a perfect emulsion. Leave to cool to room temperature.

Pour the glaze into a clean bowl or food container, cover and refrigerate for 12 hours. Reheat the refrigerated glaze to 27–30°C before using.

MERINGUE KISSES

MAKES ABOUT 60

100g egg whites
a pinch of salt
100g caster sugar
50g icing sugar, sifted

You will also need
Piping bag fitted with a 5mm plain nozzle

Heat the oven to 100°C fan. Line two or three large baking sheets with baking paper.

In a stand mixer fitted with the whisk, whisk the egg whites with the salt on medium speed until they will hold soft peaks. Little by little, add the caster sugar, whisking until the sugar is completely incorporated and the meringue holds stiff peaks.

Using a large spoon, one third at a time, fold in the sifted icing sugar, but take care not to over-mix.

Scoop the meringue into the piping bag fitted with a 5mm plain nozzle and pipe 2cm kisses on the lined baking sheets, spacing them evenly apart. Bake for about 1 hour or until crisp and dry.

CARAMEL SAUCE

MAKES ABOUT 950G

375g 35%-fat cream or whipping cream
75g liquid glucose
350g caster sugar
100g unsalted butter, at room temperature, cubed
4g salt
50g 35% white chocolate (such as Valrhona Dulcey), chopped

A well-made caramel sauce should carry a hint of bitterness, which comes from the caramelisation of the sugar. Adding white chocolate then lends a distinctive depth of flavour. Versatile and rich, this sauce enhances cake fillings, spreads beautifully on bread and is a brilliant indulgence drizzled over ice cream.

In a medium saucepan over a medium heat, combine the cream and glucose and bring the mixture to a boil.

Meanwhile, tip the sugar into another pan and melt it gently and evenly over a low heat without stirring. Continue cooking until the caramel is a deep amber-brown colour.

Slide the caramel off the heat and gradually and carefully add the hot cream, stirring continuously until combined.

Add the butter and salt, bring the caramel back to a boil, and continue cooking until the sauce reaches 105°C.

Remove the pan from the heat, add the chocolate and blend using a hand blender to blitz together to a perfect emulsion.

Leave the sauce to cool, then cover it and keep it at room temperature for at least 12 hours, or until needed. Use the caramel sauce within 1 week.

ANGLAISE SAUCE

200g 35%-fat cream or whipping cream
200g whole milk
40g caster sugar
80g egg yolks

In a medium saucepan over a medium heat, combine the cream and milk and bring the mixture to a boil.

In a bowl using a balloon whisk, mix together the caster sugar and egg yolks until they are combined and slightly paler in colour.

Add the hot cream and milk to the egg yolks, whisking continuously until smooth. Return the mixture to the pan, place it over a low–medium heat and cook to 84°C.

Strain the sauce into a clean bowl and sit the bowl in a sink of iced water to cool quickly to 4°C. Cover and chill until needed. Use within 48 hours.

GELATINE MASS

100g gelatine powder
500g water

Place the gelatine powder into a bowl, add the water and mix using a balloon whisk until thoroughly combined.

Cover or seal the gelatine mass in an airtight food container and chill until set. Use within 48 hours.

VANILLA CHANTILLY

MAKES ABOUT 800G

600g 35%-fat cream or whipping cream
70g caster sugar
¼ vanilla bean, halved
42g gelatine mass (see page 207)
120g mascarpone

In a small saucepan over a low–medium heat, warm half of the cream with the sugar and vanilla-bean halves until the cream reaches 60°C.

Remove the pan from the heat, add the gelatine mass and stir until thoroughly melted and combined. Strain the mixture through a fine-meshed sieve into a clean bowl. Add the remaining cream and the mascarpone and use a hand blender to blitz the mixture until smooth.

Leave the Chantilly to cool, then cover it and chill it for 12 hours or overnight before using. Use within 3 days.

Just before use, whip the cream until thickened to the required consistency.

CRÉMEUX-BASED GANACHES

GUANAJA CHOCOLATE

MAKES ABOUT 500G

8g caster sugar
2g pectin X58
190g 70% dark chocolate, such as Valrhona Guanaja, chopped
150g whole milk
100g 35%-fat cream or whipping cream
45g liquid glucose

In a small bowl, mix together the sugar and pectin to combine.

Melt the chocolate in a heatproof bowl over a pan of barely simmering water, stir until smooth and remove from the heat.

In a small saucepan, heat the milk, cream and glucose over a low–medium heat to 45°C. Add the sugar and pectin mixture, stir to combine, bring to a boil, then simmer for 10 seconds.

Pour the milk mixture into the melted chocolate and mix using a hand blender until the ganache is shiny and thoroughly emulsified.

The ganache will keep in an airtight container in the fridge for up to 1 week. Leave it at 18°C (room temperature) for 12 hours or overnight before using.

JIVARA MILK CHOCOLATE

MAKES ABOUT 600G

8g caster sugar
2g pectin X58
300g 40% milk chocolate, such as Valrhona Jivara, chopped
35g cocoa butter
150g whole milk
100g 35%-fat cream or whipping cream

In a small bowl, mix together the sugar and pectin to combine.

Melt the chocolate and cocoa butter in a heatproof bowl over a pan of barely simmering water, stir until smooth and remove from the heat.

In a small saucepan, heat the milk and cream over a low–medium heat to 45°C. Add the sugar and pectin mixture, stir to combine, bring to a boil, then simmer for 10 seconds.

Pour the milk mixture into the melted chocolate and mix using a hand blender until the ganache is shiny and thoroughly emulsified.

The ganache will keep in an airtight container in the fridge for up to 1 week. Leave it at 18°C (room temperature) for 12 hours or overnight before using.

OPALYS WHITE CHOCOLATE

MAKES ABOUT 650G

8g caster sugar
2g pectin X58
340g 33% white chocolate, such as Valrhona Opalys, chopped
45g cocoa butter
150g whole milk
100g 35%-fat cream or whipping cream

In a small bowl, mix together the sugar and pectin to combine.

Melt the chocolate and cocoa butter in a heatproof bowl over a pan of barely simmering water, stir until smooth and remove from the heat.

In a small saucepan, heat the milk and cream over a low–medium heat to 45°C. Add the sugar and pectin mixture, stir to combine, bring to a boil, then simmer for 10 seconds.

Pour the milk mixture into the melted chocolate and mix using a hand blender until the ganache is shiny and thoroughly emulsified.

The ganache will keep in an airtight container in the fridge for up to 1 week. Leave it at 18°C (room temperature) for 12 hours or overnight before using.

CREAM-BASED GANACHES

Use these ganaches to fill macaroons or even to pour into a tart shell and leave to set. Ideally, serve them at room temperature for a smooth, melting, fondant effect.

GUANAJA CHOCOLATE

MAKES ABOUT 600G

235g 35%-fat cream or whipping cream
60g liquid glucose
260g 70% dark chocolate (such as Valrhona Guanaja), chopped
30g unsalted butter, cubed, at room temperature

In a small saucepan, heat the cream and glucose together over a low–medium heat to 80°C.

In a heatproof bowl set over a pan of barely simmering water, melt the chocolate to 45°C. Remove the bowl from the heat.

Pour half of the cream into the chocolate and mix with a rubber spatula to combine. Add the remaining cream and blitz using a hand blender to fully emulsify the mixture to a smooth ganache.

Leave the ganache to cool to 35–40°C, then add the butter and mix again using the hand blender to make a perfect emulsion.

The ganache will keep in an airtight container in the fridge for up to 1 week. Leave it at 18°C (room temperature) for at least 24 hours before use.

JIVARA MILK CHOCOLATE

MAKES ABOUT 600G

175g 35%-fat cream or whipping cream
40g liquid glucose
330g 40% milk chocolate (such as Valrhona Jivara), chopped
40g unsalted butter, cubed, at room temperature

In a small saucepan, heat the cream and glucose together over a low–medium heat to 65°C.

In a heatproof bowl set over a pan of barely simmering water, melt the chocolate to 40°C. Remove the bowl from the heat.

Pour half of the cream into the chocolate and mix with a rubber spatula to combine. Add the remaining cream and blitz using a hand blender to fully emulsify the mixture to a smooth ganache.

Leave the ganache to cool to 35–40°C, then add the butter and mix again using the hand blender to make a perfect emulsion.

The ganache will keep in an airtight container in the fridge for up to 1 week. Leave it at 18°C (room temperature) for at least 24 hours before use.

OPALYS WHITE CHOCOLATE

MAKES ABOUT 600G

150g 35%-fat cream or whipping cream
40g glucose
365g 33% white chocolate (such as Valrhona Opalys), chopped
30g unsalted butter, cubed, at room temperature

In a small saucepan, heat the cream and glucose together over a low–medium heat to 65°C.

In a heatproof bowl set over a pan of barely simmering water, melt the chocolate to 40°C. Remove the bowl from the heat.

Pour half of the cream into the chocolate and mix with a rubber spatula to combine. Add the remaining cream and blitz using a hand blender to fully emulsify the mixture to a smooth ganache.

Leave the ganache to cool to 35–40°C, then add the butter and mix again using the hand blender to make a perfect emulsion.

The ganache will keep in an airtight container in the fridge for up to 1 week. Leave it at 18°C (room temperature) for at least 24 hours before use.

WHIPPING GANACHES

These whipped ganaches will give you the lightness of a freshly whipped cream and the stability to hold firm. The trick is to leave the ganaches in the fridge overnight and to whip to the desired texture only when you are ready to use.

For the starch base (applicable to all)
220g whole milk
7g potato starch
15g liquid glucose

In a small bowl, whisk one third of the milk with the potato starch until smooth. Set aside.

Heat the remaining milk and the glucose in a small saucepan over a low–medium heat to 85°C.

Slide the pan off the heat and add the starch mixture. Whisk until smooth. Return the pan to the heat, bring the mixture to a boil, then simmer for at least 30 seconds to thicken and cook out the starch. Use immediately.

DARK CHOCOLATE

MAKES ABOUT 400G

130g 68% dark chocolate (such as Valrhona Nyangbo), chopped
200g starch base, hot
100g 35%-fat cream or whipping cream

Tip the chocolate into a bowl and pour over the hot starch base. Using a hand blender, blitz the mixture to a perfect emulsion.

Add the cream and blend again until smooth. Cover and leave in the fridge for at least 12 hours before using. Use within 1 week.

Just before using, whisk the ganache to the desired consistency.

MILK CHOCOLATE

MAKES ABOUT 450G

150g 53% milk chocolate (such as Valrhona Hukambi), chopped
25g gelatine mass (see page 207)
200g starch base, hot
100g 35%-fat cream or whipping cream

Melt the chocolate in a heatproof bowl over a pan of barely simmering water, then remove the bowl from the heat.

Add the gelatine mass to the hot starch base and mix to combine and melt the gelatine. Add this to the melted chocolate and use a hand blender to blitz the mixture to a perfect emulsion.

Add the cream and blend again until smooth. Cover and leave in the fridge for at least 12 hours before using. Use within 1 week.

Just before using, whisk the ganache to the desired consistency.

WHITE CHOCOLATE

MAKES ABOUT 500G

170g 33% white chocolate (such as Valrhona Opalys), chopped
25g gelatine mass (see page 207)
200g starch base, hot
130g 35%-fat cream or whipping cream

Melt the chocolate in a heatproof bowl over a pan of barely simmering water. Stir until smooth, then remove the bowl from the heat.

Add the gelatine mass to the hot starch base and mix to combine and melt the gelatine. Add this to the melted chocolate and use a hand blender to blitz the mixture to a perfect emulsion.

Add the cream and blend again until smooth. Cover and leave in the fridge for at least 12 hours before using. Use within 1 week.

Just before using, whisk the ganache to the desired consistency.

INDEX

This book would not have been possible without the hugely talented teams, Front and Back of House, who have upheld the highest standards of Afternoon Tea at Langham Hotels in London and around the world for 160 years and counting. Thank you for your continued creativity, talent, passion and drive to Build Great Memories for our guests.

To Chefs Andrew Gravett, Sean Hu, Berwyn Davies and Roy Ma whose passion, precision and generosity of recipes have brought this book to life – thank you for your hard work and trust without which this book would not have been possible.

Thank you also to Bob van den Oord, Stefan Soennichsen and Michel Roux Jr for their support and to Shelley Tso, Janette Choi and Pierre Pang for their insight and guidance.

Finally, appreciation and credit to team Quarto for their inspiration, good taste, exceptional eye for composition and detail – Jessica Axe, Emma and Alex Smith, Jamie Orlando Smith, Judy Barratt and Annie Rigg.

Happy Cooking!
Chris King, VP Food and Beverage

MIX
Paper | Supporting responsible forestry
FSC® C016973

Quarto

First published in 2026 by White Lion Publishing, an imprint of The Quarto Group.
One Triptych Place, London, SE1 9SH, United Kingdom
T (0)20 7700 9000
www.Quarto.com

EEA Representation, WTS Tax d.o.o., Žanova ulica 3, 4000 Kranj, Slovenia
www.wts-tax.si

A catalogue record for this book is available from the British Library.

ISBN 978-1-80570-140-8
Ebook ISBN 978-1-80570-141-5

10 9 8 7 6 5 4 3 2 1

Design and Art Direction Smith & Gilmour
Project Editor Judy Barratt
Photographer Jamie Orlando Smith
Recipe Consultant Annie Rigg
Publisher Jessica Axe
Editor Róisín Duffy
Senior Designer Renata Latipova
Senior Production Controller Rohana Yusof

Printed in Guangdong, China TT112025